STRENGTH for *Your* JOURNEY

These writings are a mere glimpse of what the Lord has taught me on my own life's journey. I am so aware of the fact that God, in His great mercy, has been with me every step of the way: guiding me, healing me, forgiving me, inspiring me, teaching me, holding me, and loving me.

I pray that you, too, may experience God's presence as you take this journey with me.

Linda Rose

Linda Rose
Certified Spiritual Director/Companion
linda@lindarose.biz/Email
www.lindarose.biz/website
www.facebook.com/strenghforyourjourneydevotional
St. Gregory the Great Catholic Church
200 North University Dr. Plantation, FL 33324

Cover Design:
Derek Perez Design, Derek Perez, CEO-DESIGNER
Graphic Web Designer
www.derekperezdesign.com

Illustrations:
Morse Arts & Crafts - Michelle R. Morse - Muralist & Illustrator
www.mmorse.com

Create Space Independent Publishing Platform, North
Charleston, SC
LCCN 2015905384

—

Imprimatur and ***Nihil Obstat***:
Most Reverend Thomas Wenski
Archbishop of Miami, Florida
June 12, 2015
Msgr. Chanel Jeanty
Chancellor

ARCHDIOCESE OF MIAMI

Office of the Archbishop

Decree

THOMAS G. WENSKI

by the grace of God and favor of the Apostolic See
Archbishop of Miami

The text *"Strength for your Journey"* has been carefully reviewed and found free of anything which is contrary to the faith or morals as taught by the Roman Catholic Church.

Therefore, in accord with canon 824 of the *Code of Canon Law*, I grant the necessary *approbatio* for the publication of *"Strength for your Journey."*

This *imprimatur* is an official declaration that this text is free of doctrinal or moral error and may be published. No implication is contained therein that the one granting this *imprimatur* agrees with the contents, opinions or statements expressed by the author of the texts.

Given in Miami, Florida, on the 12 of June in the Year of our Lord Two Thousand and Fifteen.

Archbishop of Miami

Attestatio et Nihil Obstat

Cancellarius

Letter from the Editor

Dear Reader,

As I was describing *Strength for Your Journey* recently to a friend who had not yet read it, I was asked, "So, how is *Strength for Your Journey* different from other religious texts?"

Linda Rose. That was my simple answer. The pages of this very special book are filled with practical teachings through an exclusive human account from a woman who sings for the Lord. Saint Augustine once said, "He who sings, prays twice." Linda Rose not only sings beautifully, but she has realized something vital along her life's path and purpose.

Linda has been heavily involved with the Church for most of her adult life through song and spiritual leadership, but she gained real "spiritual muscles" when she realized this simple Truth: Knowing that we are one with God intellectually is not enough. Scripture tells us, "Faith without works is dead." We must implement our spiritual practice daily for the awareness that this thing called life is simply a great adventure (a journey) that we must live in faith through service for God and others. But how?

I have been a close witness to the legendary Linda Rose's celestial vocals for many years. I am now honored to have come to work closely with Linda on this project that began just as another humble contribution to the Church as weekly devotional columns. Whether it's a warm, encouraging anecdote by Linda; a powerful, personalized Scripture verse or a compassionate reminder to "keep going", you'll find that this charming devotional reaches deeply into the heart for 52 weeks in the year.

Whether it's for you or a cherished one who needs comfort and food for the soul, share *Strength for Your Journey* that will last a lifetime.

Warmest wishes,

Diandra Garcia
Editor

Letter from Father Hoyer

We are so busy trying to keep up with the hectic pace required to get things done that we often miss out on receiving the strength and direction we need from God in order to live our lives. Our short attention spans make us restless; we want to move on to the next subject, the next show, the next appointment on our smart phones, or the next computer pop-up. This is so common that many of us don't stay focused on God for more than a fleeting *"Help me Lord"* prayer.

I asked the well-known spiritual director of St. Gregory the Great Catholic Church, Linda Rose, to write a series of columns for our weekly bulletin and then suggested she compile them into this devotional book. Many times I am asked, *"How do I live out my Christian faith?"* The answer is found when you seek stories, wisdom and insight from those who have experienced the ups and downs of the Christian walk. Linda's *STRENGTH FOR YOUR JOURNEY* can help you relate your own life experiences to Christ's as you journey in learning how to live out the Christian faith.

May these 52 devotionals, timeless truths and practical tips show you the strength for your journey. Jesus offers life, rest, and victory to those who are willing to follow Him. That is why this book is so important to us.

I thank Linda Rose for her faith commitment and sharing her insights with me, our parishioners and now with you. I encourage Linda Rose, now a bestselling author, to provide us with another inspirational work to give us super strength for our journey.

May the Holy Spirit inspire you to find strength for your year long journey with Linda Rose.

Be strong and courageous. Do not be afraid; do not be discouraged, for the Lord your God will be with you wherever you go. **Joshua 1:9**

This is what we call **STRENGTH FOR YOUR JOURNEY!**

Michael Hoyer

Reverend Michael ("Happy") Hoyer, Pastor
St. Gregory the Great Catholic Church
Plantation, Florida 33324

I will make a roadway in the wilderness... **Isaiah 43:19**

Introduction

*I will make a roadway in the wilderness... **Isaiah 43:19***

This is the message I heard deep within my heart in the midst of one of the most difficult times in my life.

For the next seven years I received many tools and revelations that helped me understand how to trust God and stand on my faith. I gradually learned how to grow into a spiritually-free soul who had the ability to act on my faith rather than react from my dysfunction.

I felt like I was in the Wilderness. My life...my dreams...all fell apart. I had no job. I was alone. I felt so abandoned and rejected. I felt worthless and afraid. All seemed dark and hopeless. I didn't know how to go on.

I had faith in God, but that didn't seem to help me...

How can your faith in God help you when your life's journey brings trauma, loss, sickness, and disappointments with so many trials?

I searched for years. I heard so many testimonies from wonderful, faith-filled people about how God guided, healed and helped them on their own life's journey. They seemed to grow into peaceful people who were strong and "had it together" in spite of their trials.

They walked in Trust! It all made sense...

However, as for me and my journey - I still didn't get it. I thought I was following God, but when it came to my life's struggles, I was lost. I didn't know how to use what I believed to attain healing, help, and - most of all - peace. I wanted joy! I wanted to be one of those people who knew how to handle life's curves without it destroying me.

In this devotional, I will share the many tools that I received from our Lord, including THE KEYS TO FREEDOM: FAITH, TRUST, OBEDIENCE AND LOVE.

You will learn how to improve your Spiritual Muscles as you enter the BOOT CAMP FOR THE KINGDOM. I will share the many revelations that our most loving and merciful God has revealed to me.

One thing has been made very clear to me: We are all on our own **unique** journey - a journey to grow into holiness...closer to God...and it takes TIME for all to unfold as we cooperate with God in what He is doing in our lives! Remember that God is good and only desires good for you.

RECOMMENDED:

Please don't read ahead. Take this devotional one week at a time. Do the prayer assignment each week and journal. This is a yearlong walk with the Lord: Be patient... persevere... ponder... take your time.

The journey is just that - A JOURNEY, *YOUR* JOURNEY. God will bring you where He wants in **His** time. There will be many bumps, distractions and interruptions along this road. But that's ok...keep going!

REMEMBER:

"For I know the plans I have for you," declares the Lord. "Plans for welfare and not for evil, to give you a future and a hope. **Jeremiah 29:11**

For I am confident of this very thing - that He who began a good work in you will perfect it until the day of Christ Jesus. **Philippians 1:6**

Steps You May Want to Take

On this Journey...

1. Find a comfortable place to sit quietly, uninterrupted. Have your *Strength for Your Journey* book open to each week's devotional. Read the devotional for the week every day for six days. Each day maintain a journal of your ponderings.

2. Ask the Lord to help you to listen with your heart. Give the Lord *Thanks and Praise.*

3. Let go of all anxiety, concerns, worries, and the lists of things that are on your mind so that this time is dedicated only for God.

4. Ask for the Holy Spirit to fall graciously upon you.

5. Meditate. In your heart, ponder what you have just read. Try to avoid your own reasoning or your own imagination and listen to the Holy Spirit deep within your soul.

6. Talk to God about what you have received in your prayer. Thank God.

7. End this prayer time with the *Our Father.*

8. Record in your journal what came up for you during the prayer. *How did you feel? Did you receive any new insights?* Maybe you did not receive anything...*journal that.*

9. On the seventh day look back over your weeks' journaling: prayerfully read and ponder what you wrote. Then repeat numbers 6-9. [1]

   * Do this for each of the 52 weeks, re-reading each week for six days and looking back on the seventh.

Now, let's begin the journey. . .

SPIRITUAL DIRECTOR

What is a Spiritual Director? A Spiritual Director is one who, with proper training, is able to help you discern God's movements in your life – a helper along your own spiritual journey!

Now, how may I help you? Well, first I'll ask you this:

What is your prayer life like? And are you seeking God's will?

OUR GUIDE

How will we know what God is saying if we are not listening? God's will is most often very different than ours!

Maybe this will help explain: Most people who know me know that I love the TV series, *Star Trek*. I just love watching as they explore strange new worlds and seek out new civilizations! They had no guide book on the ways of that new world, and this resulted in many hardships, trials, tribulations, etc.

Sound familiar?

Unlike the *Star Trek* team, we *do* have a guide book – the Bible – to show us how to live in the Kingdom of God. Jesus tells us that we are **in** this world but not **of** this world. In essence, when we follow God we are living in an alien world. I love this, don't you? **The Kingdom of God**. His ways, His laws are so opposite of humanity.

Think about it: Pray for your enemies; do good to those who hate you; thank and praise God in *all* circumstances – that means *all of the time* – plus give 10% of your work earnings back to God.

I tell you this: if you will walk in His ways and keep His commandments, you will be given the grace to walk through your life's journey. But even more: the trials and tribulations on your journey will turn into blessings!

OUR UNIQUE JOURNEY

Now, how do we do this? How do we act the complete opposite of what we have learned all of our lives? We grew up in this world, shaped by our families of origin, teachers, cultures, experiences, traumas, disappointments, etc. Much of what we have learned on our unique journeys is good, however, our actions are often a result of what we have learned in the world, and they may prohibit us from **ACTING** on God's ways. How are we able to keep God's commands when we have been broken? How do we become free to **act** on our faith rather than **react** from our brokenness?

During one of my trials some years ago, the Lord gave me some keys to help me work to that end, and I would be honored to share them with you.

These keys are **FAITH, TRUST, OBEDIENCE & LOVE!**

PRAYER ASSIGNMENT FOR WEEK 1:

Pray: Thank you, Lord, for revealing the Truth about WHAT or WHO I am following in my life.

Pray and ponder this every day for six days.

Have your journal ready and refer back to the steps on page 3.

KEYS TO FREEDOM[2]

Last week I shared with you that the Lord gave me *keys* to help along my journey through some difficult times. The *revelation* or the **knowing** that I received was that these *keys* would help me to live in Spiritual Freedom. That is, I was granted the tools to help me follow **GOD'S** ways, not mine! Another way to say this is, to *act* from my *faith*, not *react* from myself or my dysfunction.

Jesus said: *The Spirit of the Sovereign Lord is upon Me because the Lord has anointed Me: He has sent Me to bring glad tidings to the lowly, to heal the brokenhearted, to proclaim liberty to the captives and release to the prisoners.* ***Isaiah 61:1***

THE KEY OF FAITH[3]

Because I am an artistic type of person, I relate to color and images, so...

The **Key of Faith** is green. Just as the green earth is our foundation for our physical buildings: **Faith** is the foundation for the building of our spiritual life.

We fix our eyes not on what is seen but on what is unseen. ***2 Corinthians 4:18***

Remember that we are not *of* this world - we are *in* this world. We are challenged to act on our faith not react from ourselves!

My **faith** is what I have built my life upon. It is my hope, dream, and purpose. It is my healing; my comfort; my stability; my end and beginning! Without my rock of faithful living, what would be left? What is my purpose? Why am I alive?

I believe that I have been fearfully and wonderfully made... *Psalm 139:14*..... that God began a good work in me, and He will perfect it until Jesus comes.... *Philippians 1:6*... that I am gifted for the purpose of glorifying God, that God is with me always and knows me better than I know myself. So I can put all my **faith** in Him!

YOUR UNIQUE FOUNDATION

When do you first remember learning about your faith? Was there a person or people in your past that inspired you? Perhaps you grew up in an abusive situation or were the victim of trauma, loss or any number of other tragedies, unable to wrap your head around the concept of **faith**, much less God – if He is real, where was He for me? Hopelessness creeps in when we believe in an unloving God who seemed absent during challenging times.

I had a real problem with that very thing: If God is real, where was He for me? Where was He when I lost all of my material possession; my child suffered; my marriage fell apart and my dad died in a tragic boating accident?

How do I have **faith** in someone who I can't see or hear, who is supposed to love and care for me? It took lots of *decision-making* over and over again to try believing - to try to stand on **faith,** I had to look at the walls I built within myself, the false visions I had of God because of my life experience with men and various other challenges. Remember this: We are not "*of* this world, we are *in* it!"

We are to **act** on what we believe – our **faith** alone, not on our own **vision, reasoning, imagination or our brokenness...** **ASK & YOU SHALL RECEIVE.**

If you find that you just can't understand many things in your life or worry and have anxiety, anger, disappointment, fear, and you are unable to act on your **faith: ASK FOR FAITH!!!** God will give you more than you can imagine. **God will give you the Grace to look *up* and not *around*!**

PRAYER ASSIGNMENT FOR WEEK 2:

Pray: Thank you, Lord, for giving me *faith* so that I will *act* from *faith* rather than react from my dysfunction.

(Remember, you are reading this same material for a whole week...do the assignment, journal and look back on the seventh day repeating steps 6-9. Beside the prayer assignment record any other thoughts or memories that may have come up. Not to worry; you asked the Holy Spirit to be with you, and He will take care of any memory!)

AN ACT OF FAITH

I lead a musical ensemble: *Linda Rose & Company*. We, along with a ministry named *Answered Prayers Project*, were once invited to lead worship and minister to women at *The Mary Hall Freedom House* in Atlanta, Georgia.

There are four backup singers in the ensemble and three musicians. The singers and I bought airline tickets, and the three musicians planned on driving up. Well, about a week before the trip the musicians informed me that they were not able to go. Each had a good reason, but *what now?*

How will we sing without any instrumentation? Normally I would have cancelled the "gig", but four of our singers bought tickets and took days off of work to be there! In the past I would have felt guilt.... fear... embarrassment... anxiety... I would have been so stressed out... crying... thinking of what a disaster this was. *Why did I think I could do this? Who did I think I was?*

Instead I went to the Lord and affirmed, *Well, Lord, apparently You have someone else in mind that You want to have play with us. Thank You for guiding me to find that person!*

THE ANSWER

The next morning when I woke up, I had the idea to call a friend of mine in Atlanta who I had sung with in the past. When I asked her if she or another friend would be available, she informed me that it would be impossible for them, but she gave me the name of someone who might help. I called this young man, told him my story and asked if he would be available.

He said, *Sure, I am off on Mondays and would love to play for you!*

Furthermore, I asked what he does for a living - to which he replied, *I am the music minister for the Catholic Liturgies at Emory College and work part-time at St. Peter Channel Church here in Atlanta.*

Wow! God is so good He was also gracious enough to bring with him a bass player!

I didn't even mention that I couldn't even get in touch with the Founders of the *Mary Hall Freedom House* to finalize timing and the program schedule: *Could we get into the room so that the sound equipment could be delivered and we could practice?*

After all, we had not played with these musicians and didn't even know if they knew the music! *Answered Prayers Project* was also coming to set up... on and on. Needless to say, this was an experience in *acting on Faith.*

THE BLESSINGS

The blessings were incredible! Since I went to the Lord with this challenge, **I was gifted with peace and confidence that God had my back!** I even laughed at the seemingly messed up plans!

The keyboard and bass players seemed like they had played with us forever! It turned out that one of my sons played drums with us and another son sang with us! Double the blessings. The backup singers were so "on tune," and the women that attended were amazing. They stood, sang and worshiped with us. What a glorious opportunity to spread the Good News. This was so much more than I had ever expected or dreamed of.

When we *act* on our Faith... *Look up instead of around*... there is no telling what God will do!

PRAYER ASSIGNMENT FOR WEEK 3:

Remember a time when you ACTED on your FAITH.... thank God for that time and share it with someone this week! *Your prayer assignments, ponderings and journaling are so important for you!*

For the past three weeks, we have discussed walking in **The Kingdom of God**. This Kingdom is like an alien world as we are *not of this world,* we are *in this world.* We need to *act* on our **faith** not react from ourselves or our dysfunction. And to do this we must consult our guide book— **THE BIBLE!**

For my thoughts are not Your thoughts, neither are Your ways my ways, declares the Lord! ***Isaiah 55:8***

THE KEYS TO FREEDOM

KEYS: tools to help us follow God's ways not ours. The first KEY is the key of **FAITH**.

KEY of FAITH: Green... Just as the green earth is the foundation for our physical buildings; **FAITH** is the foundation for the building of our spiritual life.

Despite our false visions of God, life experiences, trials, traumas, disappointments, and failures, we need to make a decision over and over again to have **FAITH** in *His* Word, *His* ways – even when things make no sense and when circumstances become overwhelmingly painful.

Remember this: I have built my life on **FAITH** -my hopes, dreams, purpose, comfort, stability, healing... EVERYTHING! FAITH is my life's foundation!

GOD'S WORDS

Because my dysfunctional actions and thoughts have brought so much pain, failure and grief into my life, I turned to the Word of God for guidance. I made a decision to believe. The Lord gave me the grace to have **FAITH** in His Word and His ways.

I especially love the PSALMS! In them I find a roadmap for living in THE KINGDOM! In the PSALMS I find healing words, strength, guidance, and proper ways to act and think - everything I need to walk in the ways of GOD.

PSALM 23

In contemplating Psalm 23, during a time of rejection, abandonment, betrayal, shame, and loss, the Lord gave me these revelations:

The Lord is my Shepherd, I shall not want.

It is His job to supply all of my needs – food, shelter, emotional support...

He makes me lie down in green pastures: He restores my soul; He guides me in the paths of righteousness for His name's sake.

He will take all of my burdens, hurts, and brokenness to bring healing. He will guide me on the way that is aligned with His will.

Even though I walk through the valley of death, I fear no evil, for You are with me, Your rod and Your staff, they comfort me.

When I am in the pit, and I don't see any way out I must know that You are with me and that You will be my strength.

You prepare a table before me in the presence of my enemies; You have anointed my head with oil, my cup overflows.

You set the time, space, and circumstances in front of my enemies. You anoint me with your Holy Spirit and pour down Your overflowing graces so that I am able to love like You.

Surely goodness and loving kindness will follow me all the days of my life!

When I obey and do what God wants me to do, goodness and kindness will be with me always and in all ways.

And I will dwell in the house of the Lord forever.

When I walk with the Lord in his Kingdom, I am eternal

PRAYER ASSIGNMENT FOR WEEK 4:

Thank the Lord for giving you FAITH and for speaking to your heart. Go to the Bible and spend time reading and contemplating His Words to you!

Pray...Ponder...Journal!

You made the first month! You deserve a break. Take time to rest and relax.

While you rest, look prayerfully back on your month's journaling...

WEEK 5

KEY OF TRUST[4]

Crystal – the perfect diamond – is truly crystal clear, harder than steel and flawless. One who trusts the Lord sees through his or her daily trials as if they were transparent. Through those trials, they see the Lord's abiding love. They see that trust in Him is perfect, flawless and are not easily broken.

TRUST TAKES TIME

Trust, in my experience, takes time; 30 LONG YEARS, in my case!

When I came to the Lord 30 years ago, I delved into Scripture. I was so hungry for God's Word! At that time I was walking through one of the hardest trials of my life: I gave birth to a son who had multiple heart defects, and I was told that he would die before he was five months old. In my sorrow and struggle, I turned to God for some sense to all of it.

Little by little, I had enough faith to try God at His Word; to trust, to stand firm on, to believe in His words; to **trust** that his words are true! Words like:

Do not worry about anything, but in everything by prayer and supplication, with thanksgiving – let your requests be made known to God. And the peace of God, which passes all understanding (Because His ways are not ours!) will guard your hearts and your minds in Christ Jesus. **Philippians 4:6-7**

As I read the Scripture, *trusted* His Words to be true, *acted* on them and *believed* in them, **trust** grew in my heart. I used my *Faith* key and made the decision again and again to believe in God's ways...not mine!

As I decided to **trust** God's words, He blessed me with endurance, wisdom, hope, peace and that blessed assurance that He was with me, understood me, cared for me, would heal me and be with me no matter what happened to my son.

I actually got to the point, within my heart, where I knew that God loved my son more than I ever could, and if He decided to take him home (heaven), I knew it was for my son's ultimate good! I actually attained peace with it!

GOD'S DOING

Psalm 143:5 ...Meditate on My doings...

As the years went on, I accumulated a long journal of **"God's Doings"** in my life. I wrote what was happening in my life; that is, my joys, sorrows, hurts, and praises. Scripture reading became a part of my life as I found answers in God's word – hope, support, healing, joy, grace, council, guidance, and so much more! I recorded all of it in my journals.

They became journals of "**God's Doings**" (**God's Words in action)** in my life, and this has been a great gift to me! These *doings* are very valuable because when I doubt - when I look around and not up - when I act on my dysfunction, I have my journal, and I look back and **"meditate on God's doings"** to help me remember what God has done for me. It is then that I realize **MY GOD CAN BE TRUSTED!**

HIS WORDS ARE TRUE.

PRAYER ASSIGNMENT FOR WEEK 5:

Thank God that He is trustworthy. Think of a circumstance in your life where you need to trust God and read His word.

Some Scripture verses that may help are: Psalm 18:2, Psalm 25: 1- 2, Psalm 37:5, Proverbs 3:5, Proverbs 30:5, Isaiah 26:30, John 14:1-3.

TRUST GROWS OVER TIME

Think about this: How do you know that someone is trustworthy? Who do you know in your life that can be trusted? Now I know that we are all human and make mistakes, but I think you know what I am asking. The person who is trustworthy is someone who shows you, not only with words, but by his or her **consistent actions** over time that you can place your confidence and feel secure with them. Anyone can talk, but follow your talk with actions **time after time**, and then you can be counted as trustworthy!

DO NOT PLACE YOUR TRUST IN:

*Weapons...**Psalm 44:6**...Wealth....**Psalm 49:6-7**...Leaders...**Psalm 146:3**...Man...**Jeremiah 17:5**...Works...**Jeremiah 48:7**...One's own righteousness...**Ezekiel 33:13**.*[5]

Maybe you are like me, and you have been deeply wounded by life's many trials without placing trust in God. Maybe you have placed your trust in money, your job, your spouse, your traditions, your dreams and any number of other things. You might do this simply because it is what you have been taught, or maybe it is a defense mechanism. Whatever the reason, if you aren't placing your trust in God...His Word...Christ...you will continue having a false sense of security.

INSTEAD...PLACE YOUR TRUST IN:

*GOD'S NAME... **Psalm 33:21**... GOD'S WORD...**Psalm 119:42**... CHRIST...**Matthew 12:17-21**.*[6]

How do you begin to trust in a God who is seemingly absent from your vision and life, especially when you have been broken by life's trials? I don't know what the answer is for you, but I can only say what happened for me.

The root of my own brokenness and dysfunction is fear, which I learned growing up. Fear has taken on various forms and has led me to many dark places over the years.

In those times of desolation – those times when I couldn't feel God or believe He was there and I was loved. I somehow had the grace to reach out to God. Each time He answered me. It was His grace - His unmerited, abundant, and merciful love for me! I used my **TRUST KEY.** I immersed myself in the Scriptures – God's words to me and I began taking God at His WORD. Over time I got to know my God personally and realized that he is trustworthy.

PRAYER ASSIGNMENT FOR WEEK 6:

Thank God for giving you the grace to see the truth about who you place your trust in. Then thank God for those people...you may even want to thank them!

Always refer back to the steps on page 3.

TRUST AS A CHILD

Think of the innocence of a little child. They don't worry about what they will eat or wear. They don't worry about how they will have money to buy all the necessities; in fact, they don't worry because they **TRUST!**

Children trust that their caregiver will meet all of their needs. They don't rely on their own reasoning, dreams, imaginations, or experiences. They live in total trust.

This, my fellow followers in Christ, is exactly what we are ***commanded*** *to do.*

JESUS SAID:

THE KINGDOM OF HEAVEN IS AT HAND. ***MATTHEW 10:7***

TRULY, I SAY TO YOU, UNLESS YOU TURN AND BECOME LIKE CHILDREN, YOU WILL NEVER ENTER THE KINGDOM OF HEAVEN. ***MATTHEW 18:3-4***

MY KINGDOM IS NOT OF THIS WORLD... ***JOHN 18:36***

BEYOND WHAT THE EYES COULD SEE

You cannot see what God is doing in your life. You cannot see the Lord's abiding love for you in the midst of your trials if you don't trust Him as a child! When you look around at the circumstances - at the world - and use **your** reasoning, **your** imaginations, **your** judgments, you are simply not trusting God. You are leaning on **your own** understanding.

How can we figure Him out? God sees all of eternity! God knows us inside and out because He made us. He sees our beginning and end and everything in between. He already *knows* what we need to help us to grow in holiness.

He wants us to grow in holiness so that we may be close to Him...be more like Him...and spend all of eternity with Him.

AND HE ALLOWS "HAPPENINGS" IN OUR LIVES FOR THE GOOD! GOD IS GOOD ALL THE TIME! THE ENTIRE TIME GOD IS GOOD!

A GREAT HOMILY

Years ago, I heard one of the best homilies I've ever heard on the subject of trusting God.

The priest said, *When we finally meet our Lord in heaven we'll look into His eyes and say this: OH, THAT'S WHY I WAS BORN INTO THAT FAMILY! THAT'S WHY I WENT TO THAT SCHOOL! THAT'S WHY MY FATHER DIED WHEN HE DID! THAT'S WHY I HAD CANCER! THAT'S WHY I MARRIED THAT PERSON! THAT'S WHY I BROKE MY LEG! THAT'S WHY I WAS ABANDONED.*

The priest went on for about 20 minutes, and as he recited the seemingly never ending list of **"OH'S!"** I began crying as I realized that there was a reason for everything that happened and will continue to happen in my lifetime. And it is all meant for my ultimate good.

Now, don't misunderstand me. I am not saying that God sits up there and makes horrible things happen to us, but I do believe that *ALL THINGS WORK TOGETHER FOR GOOD TO THOSE WHO LOVE GOD.*
Romans 8:28.
God, in His divine Providence, unfailing, merciful and abiding love for us will turn it **ALL to GOOD!**

THANKFULNESS

About a year ago, I had a revelation. If I say that I truly trust God with everything then I should be thankful in all things. So I decided to change my prayers from asking to thanking Him!

The results were, and still are, amazing! When I thank God I am telling Him that I trust Him completely. I am assured that whatever the circumstance - whatever the trial - He will work it out for my good. I have learned that my God is trustworthy as time after time He has been faithful to His Word.

I am able to see through my daily trials as if they were transparent. And I am not easily broken.

Here are some of the benefits of trusting the Lord:

JOY...PSALM 5:11, **DELIVERANCE**...PSALM 22:4-5, **TRIUMPH**...PSALM 25;2-3, **LOVING-KINDNESS**...PSALM 32:10, **PROVISION**...PSALM 37:3-5, **BLESSEDNESS**...PSALM 40:4, **SAFETY**...PSALM 56: 4,11, **GUIDANCE**...PROVERBS, 3:5-6 **INHERITANCE**...ISAIAH 57:13.[7]

[Please note that the homilist was Pastor Michael "Happy" Hoyer from my home parish – St. Gregory the Great in Plantation, Florida.]

PRAYER ASSIGNMENT FOR WEEK 7:

In your prayer time, try *thanking* God for whatever you *ask* of Him: Furthermore, thank Him in every "happening" throughout your day!

Journal, journal and journal some more! Follow the steps on page 3.

OUR MOTHER MARY

Although I am Roman Catholic by birth, I did not grow up in the church. When I finally decided to search out my faith, I did so in many other churches before returning to the Catholic Church.

I was misinformed when it came to Mary, the Mother of God. It has been a long journey discovering one of the most beautiful gifts given to us by Our Lord in Our Blessed Mother. In recent years, she has been holding my broken heart in her loving hands and helping to heal it. She has also been guiding and teaching me the ways of God's Kingdom!

Mother Mary has so much wisdom, gentleness, love, knowledge, and power...

She is a most perfect model for us in the practice of putting our **trust** in God.

MARY'S CHILD-LIKE TRUST

Think about it - An angel comes to Mary and tells her she will have a son by the Holy Spirit; this child will be God's own son, and His name will be Jesus.

Mary says OK.

Wow! She doesn't freak out about the fact that she is not yet married and could be put to death! All of **her** plans for her own life were changed in an instant. How many of us would accept a change in **our** plans that readily?

I know...you think...*But she saw an angel.* And I say to you...*Even when you hear God - do you listen?*

I sure don't. But I am learning to!

It is that childlike trust that we must have if we are to walk the ways of God... follow and trust in Him... and not ourselves.

Mary trusted God all the way to Bethlehem where she gave birth to the Savior of the world! I had a revelation about this holy of nights and realized that the wise men brought all those expensive gifts to Mary and Joseph *before* they knew they would be needing money to travel to Egypt.

Remember: In a dream, God told Joseph to run to Egypt with the baby so that Jesus' life would be saved from the king who was killing all infants.

GOD INSTRUCTS HIS FOLLOWER TO DO SOMETHING, PROVIDES THE WAY TO DO IT AND IT IS DONE. JOSEPH TRUSTED AND ACTED ON IT!

REBELLION IS THE OPPOSITE OF TRUST

I can't find a Scripture anywhere that says Mary fought any of the "HAPPENINGS" in her life even when she witnessed the brutal death of her son. Now that is childlike trust!

Think of a time when you were young and wanted to play with something dangerous. That pocket knife, maybe? Matches? Your parents said *no,* and you were so upset you felt like you could handle it but your parents loved you so much they knew you were not ready to handle knives or matches. They wanted to keep you safe!

That is how our Father in heaven is with us. He knows what is dangerous. He knows what we need for our safety...for our growth.... He only wants good for us! He loves us! **HE IS TRUSTWORTHY!**

When we rebel against the "happenings" in our lives - whether large or small - we are rejecting the good that God has for us. Again, we are using *our* judgments...*our* imaginations...*our* wills...instead of **trusting** God.

PRAYER ASSIGNMENT FOR WEEK 8:

Thank God for showing you all the ways that you rebel against His will for you. Then RECEIVE the gift of TRUST that He wants to give you!

Journal some ways in which you are able to RECEIVE this grace.

It's time for rest and relaxation. You have gone for two months now...look back at your journaling.

Are you experiencing a difference in your attitude towards your life...Faith or Trust? If so, great! If not...that's ok, too, JUST KEEP GOING!

WEEK 9

KEY OF OBEDIENCE[8]

Deep blue is the color of the ocean. Without water all life withers and dies. Likewise, without obedience, our spiritual life withers and dies. We must be ready to submit our will to the Lord and say, *YOUR* WILL be done if we wish to feed our spiritual life and keep it alive. Obedience is, oddly enough, a key to freedom.[8]

OBEDIENCE

Obedience is submission to authority. In our case, it is submission to God. I have found this very difficult to follow. I was used to doing my own thing! I never really thought about the fact that I was following my own desires, dreams, and imaginations.

I just went on with my life and kept running into trouble! When I finally found the Lord, rather when He finally got my attention, I began to read the Scripture and realize that I needed to follow God's ways and not mine! I had to be submissive to Him...to OBEY His Word...to keep His commands!

IF YOU LOVE ME, YOU WILL KEEP MY COMMANDS. **John 14:15**

Keeping the Lord's commandments means to hold or observe God's commands firmly – to obey.

This, my brothers and sisters, is the *work*. This is Spiritual Exercise! If you want to become physically fit, commitment to an exercise routine is a must. If you want to live in spiritual freedom and follow God's will, a commitment to spiritual exercise is a must. Setting a regular time aside for prayer; reading God's word, asking the Holy Spirit to enlighten you;

listening with your heart to "hear" what God is saying and practicing obedience.

This takes time and effort, but the results are awesome for your soul! If you will take the time and commit to these exercises, you will be able to **walk the walk**, not just talk it. And don't forget: Act on God's ways, and don't react from yours. Then you will be spiritually free!

MY FIRST EXPERIENCE IN OBEDIENCE

My son was four years old and getting ready for his fourth experimental open heart procedure. The doctors informed me that he had a 15% chance of survival. As you can imagine, I was beside myself and could not imagine myself taking my son by the hand to lead him to what could be his death. The night before, in my sorrow and torment, I went to the scriptures and came upon:

IN ALL THINGS GIVE THANKS; FOR THIS IS GOD'S WILL FOR YOU IN CHRIST JESUS. **1 Thessalonians 5:18.**

The word *all* stood out. GIVE THANKS IN **ALL** THINGS! I found it hard to believe that God would ask me to thank Him for **everything** in my present situation. In my desperation, I decided to try it. I began thanking God that I had food and a place to live. Then I thanked Him for the hospital, doctors and their abilities and training.

I began giving thanks for my son's life as I got closer and closer to the idea of thanking God for this situation. I finally said the words, *Thank you, Father, for what is happening in my son's life!*

I fell asleep with those words on my lips, exhausted from hours of crying, agonizing and searching the scriptures. When I awoke the next morning I had **PEACE**!

I was filled with **GRACE**! It was as if I'd not just gone through all that turmoil the night before.

I had *THE PEACE THAT PASSES ALL UNDERSTANDING...* ***Philippians 4:7***

I was able to be strong for my son - to speak peacefully with him and calm him. I was able to stay with him as he fell asleep for the surgery. It was such a blessing.

PRAYER ASSIGNMENT FOR WEEK 9:

Think of a situation in your life that is not going exactly as you would like it to; thank God for it.

I know this may be hard to do. But, trust me...just say the words and leave the rest to God...say these words every day for the six days. Then look back over your week on the seventh.

WEEK 10

BOOT CAMP FOR THE KINGDOM OF HEAVEN[9]

In a similar way the spiritual exercises are like sessions of a boot camp program. Our commanding officer is God. We need to *obey His commands.* But how will we know what His commands are if we aren't listening to His words then practicing to ACT on them!

We need to have a personal relationship with our Father in heaven, and having a relationship with anyone takes time... time to talk and time to listen... time to share our lives... our hopes, dreams, joys, hurts, etc. In our spiritual lives, this is called PRAYER.

Prayer is the essence of our spiritual exercise that we must commit to on a regular basis. Think of it as though you are in boot camp for the armed forces. You will need to be physically fit for your tasks ahead, so must you be spiritually fit for your life's journey, which is your **task** here on earth.

PERSONAL RELATIONSHIP

I explained this to my children - *You could tell me about a friend of yours, what color hair they have, if they are tall, lean, heavy set or in between. And if you share the way they laugh and the things they are noted for, I will get a better picture of them in my mind.*

It is when I meet them PERSONALLY that I see if the picture I had of them is accurate or not. I can tell you that nine times out of ten it is not. When I meet them face to face, I say to myself...*Wow, that is not how I pictured them at all!*

It is like that with our Father. Until you meet Him face to face and have a PERSONAL ENCOUNTER with Him, you will not *know* Him or the things He has to say to you or what He has for you in this life and the life to come!

LETTER TO YOU FROM GOD

My Child,

You may not know Me, but I know everything about you. (Psalm 139:1) I know when you sit down and when you rise up. (Psalm 139:2) I am familiar with all your ways (Psalm 139:3) even the very hairs on your head are numbered. (Matthew 10:29-31) For you were made in My image. (Genesis 1:27) In Me you live and move and have your being (Acts 17:28) for you are my offspring. (Acts17:28) I knew you even before you were conceived. (Jeremiah 1:4-5) I chose you when I planned creation. (Ephesians 1:11-12) You were not a mistake, for all your days are written in My book. (Psalm 139:15-16) I determined the exact time of your birth and where you would live. (Acts17:26) You were fearfully and wonderfully made. (Psalm 139:14) I knit you together in your mother's womb. (Psalm 139:13) And I brought you forth on the day you were born. (Psalm 71:6) I have been misrepresented by those who don't know Me. (John 8:41-44) I am not distant and angry, but am the complete expression of love (1 John 4:16) and it is My desire to lavish My love on you (1 John 3:1) simply because you are My child and I am your Father. (1 John 3:1) I offer you more than your earthly father ever could (Matthew 7:11) for I am the perfect Father. (Matthew 5:48) Every good gift that you receive comes from My hand (James 1:17) for I am your provider and I meet all your needs. (Matthew 6:31-33) My plan for your future has always been filled with hope (Jeremiah 29:11) because I love you with an everlasting love. (Jeremiah 31:3) My thoughts toward you are countless as the sand on the seashore. (Psalm 139:17-18) And I rejoice over you with singing. (Zephaniah 3:17) I will never stop doing good to you (Jeremiah 32:40) for you are My treasured possession. *(Exodus 19:5)* I desire to establish you with all My heart and all My soul. *(Jeremiah 32:41)* And I want to show you great and marvelous things. *(Jeremiah 33:3)* If you seek Me with all your heart, you will find Me. *(Deuteronomy 4:29)* Delight in Me and I will give you the desires of your heart *(Psalm 37:4)* for it is I who gave you those desires. *(Philippians 2:13)* I am able to do more for you than you can possibly imagine *(Ephesians 3:20)* for I am your greatest encourager. *(2 Thessalonians 2:16-17)* I am also the Father who comforts you in all your troubles. *(2 Corinthians 1:3-4)* When you are brokenhearted, I am close to you. *(Psalm 34:18).* As a shepherd carries a lamb; I have carried you close to my heart. *(Isaiah 40:11)* One day I will wipe away every tear from your eyes *(Revelation 21:3-4)* and I will take away all the pain you have suffered on this earth. *(Revelation 21:3-4)* I am your Father and I love you even as I love My son, Jesus *(John 17:23)* for in Jesus, My love for you is revealed. *(John 17:26)* He is the exact representation of My being. *(Hebrews 1:3)* He came to demonstrate that I am for you, not against you *(Romans 8:31)* and to tell you that I am not counting your sins. *(2 Corinthians 5:18-19)* Jesus died so that you and I could be reconciled. *(2 Corinthians 5:18-19)* His death was the ultimate expression of My love for you. *(1 John 4:10)* I gave up everything I loved that I might gain your love. *(Romans 8:31-32)* If you receive the gift of My son Jesus, you receive Me *(1 John 2:23)* and nothing will ever separate you from My love again. *(Romans 8:38-39)* Come home and I will throw the biggest party heaven has ever seen. *(Luke 15:7)* I have always been Father, and will always be Father. *(Ephesians 3:14-15)* My question is...will you be My child? *(John 1:12-13)* I am waiting for you. *(Luke 15:11-32)*

Love from,

Your Father, Almighty God [10]

PRAYER ASSIGNMENT FOR WEEK 10:

Read this letter and LISTEN to what God says to you...then TALK to Him.

Make sure you are following the steps on page 3.   After talking to God...journal.

40

FORGIVENESS

Let all bitterness and wrath and anger and clamor and slander be put away from you, along with all malice. Be kind to one another, tenderhearted, forgiving one another, as God in Christ forgave you. **Ephesians 4:31-32**

Wow, there is much to say about these commands, but I will focus on **forgiveness**. I don't know about you, but for me this is impossible to do without the help of God. Over the years I have prayed with many people who have gone through many devastating circumstances and traumatic events.

They have had the opportunity to obey God and forgive those who have been their abusers. Those who decide to *act* on God's word and not *react* from their "stuff" experienced much healing emotionally, spiritually and physically! They walked in *spiritual freedom*. Those who continue in their stubborn resentment stay in their heartache, torment and any number of other physical illnesses.

JESUS TOLD ME

Some years ago, I was faced with a devastating truth - My life was forever changed, all of my dreams gone as I witnessed my family falling apart. I experienced what St. John of the Cross describes as *"The Dark Night of the Soul."*

I was lying on the floor wrenched with heartache, crying out to the Lord, *Jesus, how did you do it...how did you deal with the betrayal...the false accusations...fear...etc...?*

I suddenly found myself in the Garden of Gethsemane. And in the distance, I saw Jesus kneeling and praying in agony and heartache. I continued to beg for answers.

All at once in a gentle, loving manner He turned and looked straight into my eyes and said, *Linda, I knew who I was and where I was going. Feelings are not here nor there; you need to act on the truth.*

That night that beautiful revelation gave me the strength to search for myself - the Truth.

The truth is God's Word to me... and to *you*! God is real. His grace is sufficient.

Forgiveness is an act of the will, and the will can function regardless of the temperature of the heart. **-Corrie Ten Boom**

PRAYER ASSIGNMENT FOR WEEK 11:

Think of those who you need to forgive and list them in your journal. Ask God to give you the grace to OBEY His command and be able to say the words: *I FORGIVE THEM.*

This is another tough area for some of us. Remember, you don't need to FEEL the forgiveness...just OBEY. Say the words.

Hint: You may need to forgive yourself as well.

WEEK 12

Father forgive them, for they know not what they are doing.
Luke 23:34

Forgiveness. This is so hard, yet it is commanded of those dedicating their lives to following Jesus. This is the work (the spiritual exercises) we are required to obey!

Why is it so hard? Is it because of **our judgment?**

After all, we say, *They were so wrong in what they did or said...everyone agrees!*

Is it because of **our pride?** Does it have to do with **our shame, fears, past traumas?**

The issue of resentment usually has a root in us and we are so **unaware** of it. We can't forgive because of our own dysfunction; our **own will** gets in the way. **WE DO NOT KNOW WHAT WE ARE DOING!**

The results are devastating to others and to us! We hurt and destroy ourselves and each other by our hatefulness, and then we blame **THEM**!

DO NOT MISUNDERSTAND ME. YES, SOMETIMES WE ARE INNOCENT VICTIMS OF SOMEONE ELSE'S "ISSUES" BUT I AM TALKING TO YOU ABOUT **FORGIVENESS**...YOUR RESPONSE TO GOD'S COMMAND!

THE OTHER SIDE OF THE COIN

Now, on the other side, as for the person who has wronged you - how do we come to terms with what they have done or said that has hurt us so deeply and caused devastation in our lives and sometimes the lives of others? If you are using **YOUR OWN JUDGMENT...YOUR OWN SET OF RULES...YOUR OWN**

VISION AND IMAGINATION…it will be very difficult to forgive! Remember…

My thoughts are not your thoughts, neither are My ways your ways. **Isaiah 55:8**

YOUR FAITH AND TRUST KEYS

Go back to your faith and trust keys. Remember that we walk in the Kingdom of God, and it is like an alien world. We believe God's words to us…that He loves us…sees all…knows all…has mercy…heals us…protects us…guides us…makes all things right…actually works all for our good.

AND HE COMMANDS US TO BE **OBEDIENT** TO HIS WORD; **FORGIVE!**

FORGIVENESS TAKES TIME

Just because you say the words - *I forgive so and so* - does not mean that you will feel it!

Just be **OBEDIENT** and God will do the rest! You will know that the forgiveness…healing…is complete when you can see the person or circumstance as a **GIFT** in your life!

PRAYER ASSIGNMENT FOR WEEK 12:

Thank and praise God for giving you grace to practice forgiveness. Make a list of those you need to forgive in your journal. Don't forget to forgive yourself.

Keep saying I forgive so and so…look at your list…you may need to add more names!

Is it getting tougher? That is good. Remember, you are on a journey...you are in an alien world, learning how to live in it & how to walk in it. No worries though! You are not alone & you are SO LOVED!

I will stay on the **KEY of OBEDIENCE** because I believe this, my brothers and sisters, is where the real work is… and certainly where the real blessings are.

Practice submitting our wills to God's…*obeying* his Word, *keeping* His commands and *acting* on His ways, not *reacting* from ours.

This is the "boot camp" of the Kingdom of God.

TITHING

The practice of **tithing** is among one of the many **commands** we are given if we choose to live in the KINGDOM of GOD. We are to give the *first 10%* of all that we earn and are given by God…back to God. Now don't freak out! This is a wonderful thing. Listen to what the Lord says.

"Bring the whole tithe into the storehouse, that there may be food in My house, and try Me in this," says the Lord of hosts: "SHALL I NOT OPEN THE FLOODGATES OF HEAVEN TO POUR DOWN BLESSINGS UPON YOU WITHOUT MEASURE?" **Malachi 3:10**

Wow! Did you get it? Be **obedient** to the Lord, and He will POUR OUT BLESSINGS UPON YOU! Our God is challenging us. We cannot out-give our Maker!

PERSONAL EXPERIENCES

I took God up on this command some 35 years ago, and I cannot tell you how much I have been blessed. Since tithing, I have been given all that I have ever needed…a home to live in… (in spite of losing my original home)…food to eat for myself and my children…(in spite of not having an income)…clothes for myself and my children…private school education for my children...a car when mine was repossessed. Many times I was given airline tickets that enabled me to take my son to hospitals out of state for his heart surgeries...AND...I was given a few trips *just for fun*!

I have also been blessed with countless inner healings and spiritual freedoms. My list goes on and on.

God keeps pouring out blessings upon me. I do believe that it is because I keep the tithe. I am sure there were times when I slacked off a bit with this practice, but for the most part it has been a part of my life. Even if you only have one dollar, TITHE the 10%. *YES...DO IT!*

God blesses all that we give and all that we receive.

I know you will be blessed because you can never out-give God! You may also tithe your time and talent. Use your **FAITH, TRUST and OBEDIENCE KEYS then ACT on what God is commanding of you and watch what happens! Remember that God's ways are not our ways. You cannot figure out the economy of the Kingdom of God; you just have to walk in FAITH, TRUST and be OBEDIENT.**

*IN GENEROUS SPIRIT PAY HOMAGE TO THE LORD. BE NOT SPARING OF FREEWILL GIFTS. WITH EACH CONTRIBUTION SHOW A CHEERFUL COUNTENANCE AND PAY YOUR TITHES IN A SPIRIT OF JOY. GIVE TO THE MOST HIGH AS HE HAS GIVEN TO YOU, GENEROUSLY, ACCORDING TO YOUR MEANS. **Sirach 35:7-9***

*WITHOUT COST YOU HAVE RECEIVED: WITHOUT COST YOU ARE TO GIVE. **Matthew 10:8***

PRAYER ASSIGNMENT FOR WEEK 13:

Thank God for showing you the truth about tithing.

Don't forget the steps! Page 3.

WEEK 14

THE HELPER

We have already talked about some commands given by Jesus that are essential for walking in The Kingdom of God.

Things like **PRAISE AND THANK GOD IN ALL THINGS... FORGIVE... TITHE... TRUST... HAVE FAITH... OBEY**.

These things aren't natural or easy for us!

This is why The Lord sent **The Helper, The Holy Spirit; the Power Person of the Trinity** to help and empower us to be able to follow God's commands! How awesome is that! God gives commands and the power to obey them. The Holy Spirit will teach us in all truth and lead us in the ways of the Kingdom.

And I will pray to the Father, and He will give you another Helper, that He may abide with you forever, even the Spirit of truth, whom the world cannot receive, because it neither sees Him nor knows Him: but you know Him, for He dwells with you and will be in you. I will not leave you orphans: I will come to you. **John 14:16-18**

NOT OF THE WORLD

Please remember that we are not *of* this world, we are *in* it. The Kingdom of God is like an **ALIEN** world. God's ways are not our ways. His economy is not like ours! We cannot use our own imaginations, reasoning, or judgments.

We must just read His word and obey it -- The End.

ASK AND YOU SHALL RECEIVE

What stops you from obeying? Fear?... Control?... Insecurity?... Pride?

The great news is that even if you don't know, the Holy Spirit does! All you need to do is **ASK**. Remember that your Father in heaven formed you in your mother's womb. He knows you intimately - better than you know yourself.

PERSONAL EXPERIENCE

I once noticed that I was experiencing a great distance between myself and someone who I loved dearly. As time went on I became more and more distant from that person until there was a huge barrier between us. I could not explain what that barrier was nor did I think I had any part in it. Eventually the relationship ended.

In my heartache I asked the Holy Spirit: *Show me the truth and root of this.*

I did not receive an answer right away, but in God's perfect time I received my answer: I had held hurt and resentment for that person because I felt they had rejected and hurt my children.

Once I realized this, I asked the Holy Spirit for the grace and the power to obey God. I had to forgive myself, I had to forgive that person and I had to pray for God to bless that person. The Holy Spirit helped me obey, even though I did not feel like obeying! I received a great blessing, too – a deep healing and freedom within the depths of my soul.

PRAYER ASSIGNMENT FOR WEEK 14:

Pray before going to bed: *Holy Spirit, I give you permission to enter into my subconscious mind and bring me healing while I sleep.*

Journal each day...

*Be transformed by the renewing of your mind. **Romans 12:22***

RENEW YOUR MIND

I am convinced that renewing my mind; that is, thinking the way my Lord desires me to think is how to get the rest of me to **ACT** how the Lord would have me act! My mind is where my **WILL** is. I need to *submit* my will and become obedient to God to live and be **blessed** in the Kingdom of God.

However, my mind can be filled with many ungodly things - my "stuff" as I call it. This "stuff" comes from a variety of things: learned behavior from living in the world, hurts, disappointments, brokenness....BUT...

Precious in the sight of the Lord is the death of His godly ones! ***Psalm 116:15***

I love this Scripture verse because I consider the "death" as the death to myself and my "stuff". After my "stuff" fades away, then there comes the hope as God renews my mind, and I become a new creature in Christ.

I submit my will. I give up my judgments... reasoning... prejudices... anger... refusal to forgive. I will to obey and to keep God's commands. I ask Jesus to help me let go of my "stuff." I ask Jesus to heal me and show me the **root** of my dysfunction.

I use my **FAITH** and **TRUST** keys. I believe and trust Jesus when He said:

The Spirit of the Sovereign Lord is on me, because the Lord has anointed me to preach good news to the poor. He has sent me to bind up the brokenhearted, to proclaim freedom for the captives and release from darkness for the prisoners. **Isaiah 61:1**

JUST LIKE YOU

While having the revelation or *the knowing* that I wanted to die to my "stuff" and be who God wanted me to be, these words came to me in my prayer time and thus became a song!

PRAYER ASSIGNMENT FOR WEEK 15:

Pray and ponder these words all week:

SPIRIT, CHANGE MY EYES, MAKE ME SEE LIKE YOU, LET ME SEE YOUR PLAN UNFOLD, GIVE ME EYES ANEW...MAKE ME JUST LIKE YOU!

SPIRIT CHANGE MY EARS, MAKE ME HEAR LIKE YOU, LET ME LISTEN FOR YOUR VOICE IN ALL I SAY AND DO...MAKE ME JUST LIKE YOU!

MAKE ME JUST LIKE YOU, MAKE ME JUST LIKE YOU, SEND YOUR SPIRIT TO GUIDE MY LIFE, I WANT TO BE LIKE YOU...MAKE ME JUST LIKE YOU!

SPIRIT CHANGE MY MIND, MAKE ME THINK LIKE YOU, LET ME KNOW JUST WHAT TO THINK, IN ALL I SAY AND DO...MAKE ME JUST LIKE YOU!

SPIRIT CHANGE MY HEART, MAKE ME LOVE LIKE YOU, LET ME FEEL THE LOVE YOU FEEL, IN ALL I SAY AND DO... MAKE ME JUST LIKE YOU! [11]

We must be ready to submit our will to the Lord and say, *your will be done* if we wish to feed our spiritual life and keep it alive. **Obedience** is, oddly enough, another **Key to Freedom.**

Rejoice always, pray without ceasing, and give thanks in all circumstances; for this is the will of God in Christ Jesus for you. **1 Thessalonians 5:16-18**

PRAY WITHOUT CEASING

How do we pray without *ceasing*? We have jobs, children, and duties in life. Well, my brothers and sisters, we absolutely **CAN!** I am sure that you have experienced talking to someone while thinking of something else or while you are in the midst of doing something your mind may wander.

Your imagination can take you to many places in spite of where you are at the moment.

The key here is to **train** your mind to think on:

Whatever is true, whatever is noble, whatever is right, whatever is pure, whatever is lovely, whatever is admirable—if anything is excellent or praiseworthy—think about such things. **Philippians 4:8**

The concept of Boot Camp for walking in the Kingdom of God has a new meaning when we consider the training of our minds: it takes practice...desire...and a commitment to OBEDIENCE... FAITH... TRUST. Reading God's Holy Word is also **spiritual exercise.**

PRAY THE OPPOSITE

Since prayer is talking to God and my mind "talks" all day I have trained my mind to talk (pray) just the opposite of what my mind is saying. I use my FAITH and TRUST keys.

I know that God's ways are *not* my ways!

Oh, by the way, you can even "see" that when you are thinking something *not* of God. You can correct it!

It goes like this: I ride my bike to a store, park and lock it. When I come out I realize that my bike has been stolen. Immediately I say to myself, *What...That so and so person...They have some nerve, etc.*

Now at the same time I am able to **hear** my thoughts; I **see** how I am thinking. I **know** that what I am thinking is not what God would have me think and then **I DECIDE TO THINK THE OPPOSITE.**

I remember that God says to pray for my enemies, and since I am committed to following God's ways and not mine I am committed to **OBEDIENCE.** Then I surrender and say, *Okay Lord...Bless that person...They must really need a bike!*

GOD IS WITH YOU

I believe that God is with us...in us...guiding and helping us! This, my sisters and brothers, is that voice that *knowing* that helps us to discern God's ways – the awesome HOLY SPIRIT.

Likewise the Spirit helps us in our weakness. For we do not know what to pray for as we ought, but the Spirit himself intercedes for us with groanings too deep for words. **Romans 8:26**

PRAYER ASSIGNMENT FOR WEEK 16:

"Watch"..."Listen"..."Hear"...your thoughts. Thank the Holy Spirit for helping you become OBEDIENT.

Don't forget to journal.

Wow! Four months!!! Take a rest...look back over the months & notice what God is doing for you.

WEEK 17

BOOT CAMP

The practice of obedience – submitting our wills to god's will – is the **Spiritual Exercise**, the work, needed to walk and live in the KINGDOM of GOD.

OUR WILLS

Our will comes from a variety of things: dysfunctional ways of *thinking* and *acting* (learned behavior) that comes from our family of origin, culture, teachers, experiences, traumas, disappointments, rebellion, resistance, control, selfishness and any other negativity that is not of God.

Let's face it: We are human, and we are born with a sinful nature. The good news is that we have the Helper, the Holy Spirit, to help us GROW out of "ourselves" into the one God made us to be; IN HIS IMAGE!

This means: WORK... IT TAKES TIME... PRACTICE... HENCE: THE WORK!

The Spirit helps us in our weakness. For we do not know what to pray for as we ought, but the Spirit Himself intercedes for us with groaning too deep for words. **Romans 8:26**

A PRAYER FOR GROWTH

Last week we discussed the command to **PRAY WITHOUT CEASING.**

I would like to share how I pray without ceasing and practice **OBEDIENCE** so that I may become **SPIRITUALLY FREE!**

1. I RENOUNCE AND TAKE AUTHORITY OVER THE NEGATIVITY IN JESUS' NAME.

2. I ASK GOD TO FORGIVE THE MANY WAYS I COOPERATE WITH THIS NEGATIVITY.

3. I THANK GOD FOR HIS FORGIVENESS AND MERCY.

4. I RECEIVE THE BLESSINGS THAT GOD POURS OUT FOR MY LIFE AND MY DESTINY.[12]

This only takes a minute out of your day.

PERSONAL EXAMPLE

One day my friend and I had plans to go to the theater. When the time came for us to make further plans for that evening I called but got no answer. I then emailed...no response...called again...no answer...left messages... no response.

My first thought was that she had an emergency so I called one of her family members. No, she was fine. I ran into some neighbors who said they'd seen her and all seemed to be sound. Now began my dysfunctional thinking.

I am being rejected...I am not good enough for her to call me...I am angry...Why won't she tell what I did wrong?...I am betrayed...I thought she was my friend!

I imagined all sorts of things. Then I "heard" my thinking and began praying.

REJECTION, UNWORTHINESS, ANGER, GUILT, BETRAYAL -- I RENOUNCE AND TAKE AUTHORITY OVER YOU AND COMMAND YOU OUT OF MY LIFE IN JESUS' NAME.

FATHER, I ASK YOU TO FORGIVE ME FOR ALL OF THE WAYS THAT I COOPERATE WITH THIS NEGATIVITY. THANK YOU, LORD, FOR YOUR FORGIVENESS AND YOUR MERCY.

I HUMBLY RECEIVE ALL THE BLESSINGS THAT YOU POUR OUT TO ME ON MY LIFE AND MY DESTINY. AMEN.

PRAYER ASSIGNMENT FOR WEEK 17:

Watch…listen…to your thinking and reactions. Practice praying for yourself using the four steps.

Refer back to page 3. Use all the steps!

REVIEW

I have spent many weeks on the **KEY OF OBEDIENCE** with good reason. This, my sisters and brothers, is the WORK – the SPIRITUAL EXERCISE – that we need to **practice** until our minds are renewed in Christ!

THIS EXERCISE (PRACTICE) TAKES FAITH, TRUST, TIME, DEDICATION AND PERSEVERANCE. If you say that you love God and want to walk in His ways, you will need to **OBEY *HIS* WAYS** and not *yours*.

IT MAY BE ROUGH

Sometimes we don't even know why we do the things we do or say the things we say. Sometimes we don't want to look at the truth within us. I promise you that you will become **SPIRITUALLY FREE** if you submit your will to God's.

If you will use your **FAITH KEY** to believe that God is for you and not against! If you use your **TRUST KEY** just for a moment while praying, He will help you grow into the person He made you to be, a person who is **LOVED** and **GIFTED** - a child of God with a **PURPOSE.**

SCRIPTURE: GOD'S WORD

If you love Me you will keep My commands. **John 15:15**

In all things give thanks; for this is God's will for you in Christ Jesus. **1 Thessalonians 5:18**

Father, forgive them for they know not what they are doing. **Luke 23:34**

Let all bitterness and wrath and anger and clamor and slander be put away from you, along with all malice. Be kind to one another, tenderhearted, forgiving one another, as God in Christ forgave you. **Ephesians 4:31-32**

My thoughts are not your thoughts, neither are My ways your ways. **Isaiah 55:8**

Bring the whole tithe into the storehouse, that there may be food in My house, and try Me in this, says the Lord of Hosts: Shall I not open the floodgates of heaven to pour down blessings upon you without measure? **Malachi 3:10**

...I will pray the Father, and He will give you another Helper, that He may abide with you forever, even the Spirit of truth, whom the world cannot receive, because it neither sees Him nor knows Him: but you know Him, for He dwells within you and will be with you and will be in you. I will not leave you orphans: I will come to you. **John 14:16-18**

Be transformed by the renewing of your mind. **Romans 12:22**

PRAYER ASSIGNMENT FOR WEEK 18:

Thank God for showing you the areas of your life where He wants to give you Spiritual freedom then make a commitment to be **obedient** to doing the work.

KEYS TO FREEDOM ARE KEYS TO THE KINGDOM

Jesus said: *The Spirit of the Sovereign Lord is upon Me because the Lord has anointed Me: He has sent Me to bring glad tidings to the lowly, to heal the brokenhearted, to proclaim liberty to the captives and release from prisoners.* **Isaiah 61:1**

A NEW REVELATION!

One of the places I visited while in the Holy Land was the region of Caesarea Philippi. This region is in the northeast section of Israel called the Golan Heights. In Israel, all of the important churches, temples, and synagogues were built on top of hills and mountains.

Caesarea Philippi is in the foothills of Mount Hermon which is in Syria. Mount Hermon is the largest mountain in the whole area. In Arabic, Mount Hermon is called "Jabal ash Shaykh" which means "Mountain of the Chief." [13]

Our guide told us that there was a pagan temple there where there would be human sacrifices. I immediately thought... *WOW, AND WE ARE FREE!*

WE WERE ALSO FREE TO BE ABLE TO READ FROM THE HOLY BIBLE IN THAT PLACE!

When Jesus went into the region of Caesarea Philippi he asked his disciples, Who do people say that the Son of Man is? They replied, Some say John the Baptist, others Elijah, still others Jeremiah or one of the prophets. He said to them, But who do you say that I am? Simon Peter said in reply, You are the Messiah, the Son of the living God. Jesus said to him in reply, Blessed are you, Simon son of Jonah. For flesh and blood has not revealed this to you, but my heavenly Father. And so I say to you, you are Peter, and upon this rock I will build my church, and the gates of hell shall not prevail against it.

I will give you the KEYS TO THE KINGDOM of heaven. Whatever you bind on earth shall be bound in heaven; and whatever you loose on earth shall be loosed in heaven. **Matthew 16:13-19**

The words **KEYS TO THE KINGDOM** jumped out at me. All at once amazing **truths and revelations** came pouring into my mind.

GOD IS THE ONE TRUE "CHIEF." WE ARE FREE - DESPITE OUR CIRCUMSTANCES, TRIALS, FEARS, STRUGGLES, TRAUMAS, CHALLENGES, HURTS, ETC., WE HAVE THE VICTORY. WE ARE SPIRITUALLY FREE.

THE GATES OF HELL AND SATAN IN ALL HIS WORKS WILL NOT PREVAIL AGAINST US.

KEYS TO THE KINGDOM *ARE* KEYS TO FREEDOM!

PRAYER ASSIGNMENT FOR WEEK 19:

Thank God for showing you the areas in your life where you need freedom and believe that you are free.

See and record all your blessings.

KEYS TO FREEDOM...KEYS TO THE KINGDOM

The keys of FAITH, TRUST, OBEDIENCE and LOVE have helped me live in **SPIRITUAL FREEDOM** over the years: to have the ability to ACT on GOD'S WAYS not REACT from my dysfunction.

My dysfunctional ways of thinking and acting come from many things: my upbringing, culture, experiences, traumas, my will, my dreams, and my imagination. As I walk in the **KINGDOM** and use the **KEYS TO FREEDOM,** I begin to grow and be SET FREE. I am **healed** of my "stuff" so that I may become who God intended me to be and be able to receive all the blessings He showers down upon me for my life and destiny.

HEALINGS IN JERUSALEM

It was absolutely awesome being in all the places where Jesus was in Jerusalem! In every place we visited we read from the Scriptures about what took place in that very spot.

Jesus' life, work and ministry were all about healing.

THE SPIRIT OF THE SOVEREIGN LORD IS UPON ME BECAUSE THE LORD HAS ANOINTED ME TO PROCLAIM FREEDOM TO CAPTIVES AND RELEASE FROM DARKNESS TO THE PRISONERS. **Isaiah 61:1**

He performed physical healings: the blind can see...the lame can walk... the sick have recovered... the deaf can hear... the dead rise!

He performed miracles of deliverance from demons: a mute man oppressed by a demon... a Gentile woman with a demoniac daughter... the epileptic boy... the blind, deaf demoniac.

And Jesus performed mass healings of the spiritual and emotional kind: Jesus' Sermon on the Mount...the Beatitudes...Preaching's about the Kingdom of Heaven and all the parables with life lessons about how to live in God's ways. He even taught us how to pray!

JESUS STILL HEALS

As I stood on that holy ground where our Lord walked and heard the recount of what He did and said from the reading of the Holy Scriptures, I was astounded by the revelation that I received. Jesus is *still* in the business of healing. This revelation was all the assurance that I needed. The confirmation was that I had, in fact, received various healings myself. I received ultimate freedom and deliverance through the spiritual exercises and used the keys of **faith, trust, obedience, and love** to help me receive.

PRAYER ASSIGNMENT FOR WEEK 20:

Ask the Holy Spirit to look back over your life with you and show you areas where you have received healings. Then thank and praise God for his unconditional love and healing that he showers upon you.

A little hint on discernment:

God's voice: stills you, leads you, reassures you, enlightens you, encourages you, comforts you, calms you, convicts you.

Satan's voice: rushes you, pushes you, frightens you, confuses you, discourages you, worries you, obsesses you, condemns you

You are doing great work! Take a break...Contemplate where you were and where you are going.

WEEK 21

The **KEY OF LOVE** is red.

The heart is the center of the body bringing forth life-giving nutrients to all of the other parts of the body. Without it, the body cannot function. So also, **LOVE** is the heart of our **SPIRITUAL BODY** – The **BODY of CHRIST**.

LOVE calls us to forget ourselves and to give freely, using all of the gifts that we have been given. Thus the body of Christ becomes a life-giving organism throughout the world.[14]

LOVE IS AN ACTION WORD

When I first did a study on **LOVE** in the Scriptures, I was very surprised to learn that love is *not* a feeling. It is a verb, an **ACTION**!

For God so loved the world that he **gave** *his only Son, that whoever believes in him should not perish but have eternal life.* **John 3:16**

To give was the action. And what an action God did for us!

Jesus' **love** is also an action.

We know love by this — that He **laid down His life** *for us; and we ought to lay down our lives for the brethren. But whoever has the world's goods and sees his brother in need and closes his heart against him, how does the love of God abide in him? Little children, let us not love with word or with tongue but in deed and truth.* **1 John 3:16-18**

Laid down His life - Another wonderful act. We are directed to lay our lives down for others. This is **love**.

LOVE IN ACTION

Some months ago I received a call from someone whose daughter was running from an abusive husband. She left with her baby.

Someone came forward and found an empty apartment for her but then she needed furniture. I told her not to worry and that God would not leave her alone. I praised and thanked God for getting her what she needed (I used my Faith and Trust Keys!).

The next day the Lord led me to someone who knew someone that worked in a facility which held some extra furniture and household items willing to give away. The amazing thing is that within a day people came forward to help with the picking up and delivery of the furniture!

When we arrived at the facility, another miracle took place. It turned out that two-of the people in charge of giving away the furniture were once in that same situation. And by the time we left we were given the entire contents of a full two bedroom apartment!

Sheets, blankets, towels, dishes, pots, lamps...everything one could ever need. We were all thanking and praising God for all of the gifts, for the open hearts of all who came to her aid, and mostly for the **LOVE,** the **ACTION** taken for this woman and her baby!

PRAYER ASSIGNMENT FOR WEEK 21:

Thank God for showing you ways to LOVE, to LAY DOWN YOUR LIFE, to ACT for the good of others!

Remember...it is important to follow the steps from page 3.

Jesus is the Greatest Example of Love.

HISTORY

God instituted animal sacrifice through the shedding of blood for the atonement of sins. He killed an animal to make clothes to cover Adam and Eve when they sinned against Him. In the book of Leviticus we learn that God gave extensive instructions on how, when, and under what circumstances animal sacrifices were to be offered to Him in atonement.

This is the Law that God gave to Moses. This Law was to continue until Christ came to offer the ultimate perfect sacrifice which made animal sacrifice no longer necessary. These animal sacrifices were only temporary. Humans continued to sin; therefore, sacrifices were done continuously in accordance with the Law.

JESUS' BLOOD SACRIFICE

Jesus died for our sins. Jesus wasn't merely human. If He was, then His sacrifice would have also been a temporary one because one human life could not possibly cover all of the multitudes of human sin. Nor could one finite human life atone for sin against an infinite God.

The only viable sacrifice must be an infinite one, which means only God Himself could atone for the sins of mankind. Only God Himself, an infinite being, could pay the penalty owed to Him. This is why God had to become a Man and dwell among men (John 1:14).

Greater love has no one than this: to lay down one's life for one's friends. **John 15:13**

No other sacrifice would suffice. Jesus, as God incarnate, sacrificed Himself. He laid down His life willingly.

In John 10, Jesus talks about His life saying, *No one takes it from me, but I lay it down of my own accord. I have authority to lay it down and authority to take it up again.* God the Son sacrificed Himself to God the Father and thereby fulfilled all the requirements of the Law:

Jesus became the blood sacrifice in atonement for our sins, and Jesus' once-for-all-time sacrifice was followed by His resurrection. He laid down His life and took it up again, thereby providing eternal life for all who would ever believe in Him and accept His sacrifice for their sins. He did this out of love for the Father and for all those the Father has given Him (John 6:37-40).[15]

For I am convinced that neither death nor life, neither angels nor demons, neither the present nor the future, nor any powers, neither height nor depth, nor anything else in all creation, will be able to separate us from the love of God that is in Christ Jesus our Lord. **Romans 8:38-39**

Whatever your journey...whatever your struggles...whatever your challenges... whatever your hurts... whatever your failures... whatever your sins...

JESUS LOVES YOU AND IS WITH YOU!!! JESUS DIED FOR YOUR SINS. JESUS HAS OVERCOME.

PRAYER ASSIGNMENT FOR WEEK 22:

PRAISE...THANKS...GIVE GLORY TO OUR RISEN LORD!

Journal...record your praises all week!

The **KEY OF LOVE**... RED...is the heart center of the body, bringing life-giving nutrients to all the other parts of the body. Without it, bodies can no longer function. Also, **LOVE** is the heart of our spiritual body: the Body of Christ. **LOVE** calls us to forget ourselves and to give freely, using all of the gifts that we have been given. Thus the Body of Christ becomes a life-giving organism throughout the world.

USING ALL THE GIFTS THAT WE HAVE BEEN GIVEN

There are different kinds of gifts, but the same Spirit distributes them. There are different kinds of service, but the same Lord. There are different kinds of working, but in all of them and in everyone it is the same God at work. Now to each one the manifestation of the Spirit is given for the common good. To one there is given through the Spirit a message of wisdom, to another a message of knowledge by means of the same Spirit, to another faith by the same Spirit, to another gifts of healing by that one Spirit, to another miraculous powers, to another prophecy, to another distinguishing between spirits, to another speaking in different kinds of tongues and to still another the interpretation of tongues. All these are the work of one and the same Spirit, and He distributes them to each one, just as He determines. For even as the body is one and yet has many members, and all the members of the body, though they are many parts, are one body, so also is Christ. 1 Corinthians 12:4-12

My friends, Jesus said, *THIS IS MY COMMANDMENT, THAT YOU LOVE ONE ANOTHER.*

Remember that **LOVE** is an **ACTION**. All of us have been graciously gifted by God and are expected to use... to act... on them for the good of others. Please do not ever think or believe that you are not gifted! Listen to Paul's words:

...Even so the body is not made up of one part but of many. Now if the foot should say, "Because I am not a hand, I do not belong to the body," it would not for that reason stop being part of the body. And if the ear should say, "Because I am not an eye, I do not belong to the body," it would not for that reason stop being part of the body. If the whole body were an eye, where would the sense of hearing be? If the whole body were an ear, where would the sense of smell be? But in fact God has placed the parts in the body, every one of them, just as he wanted them to be. If they were all one part, where would the body be? As it is, there are many parts, but one body.

The eye cannot say to the hand, "I don't need you!" And the head cannot say to the feet, "I don't need you!" On the contrary, those parts of the body that seem to be weaker are indispensable, and the parts that we think are less honorable we treat with special honor. And the parts that are unpresentable are treated with special modesty, while our presentable parts need no special treatment. But God has put the body together, giving greater honor to the parts that lacked it, so that there should be no division in the body, but that its parts should have equal concern for each other. If one part suffers, every part suffers with it; if one part is honored, every part rejoices with it.

Now you are the body of Christ, and each one of you is a part of it. **1 Corinthians 12:14-27**

PRAYER ASSIGNMENT FOR WEEK 23:

Contemplate these Scriptures then thank God for showing you your own unique gifts, fulfilling your part in His body and thank Him for leading you to LOVE others with your gifts!

THE KEYS TO FREEDOM

THE KEY OF FAITH...GREEN...Just as the green earth is the foundation for our physical buildings: **FAITH** is the foundation for the building of our **SPIRITUAL LIFE.**

THE KEY OF TRUST...CRYSTAL...The perfect diamond is truly crystal clear, harder than steel and flawless. One who **TRUSTS** the Lord sees through their daily trials as if they were transparent. Through those trials they see the Lord's abiding love. They see that **trust in Him** is perfect, flawless, and they are not easily broken.

THE KEY OF OBEDIENCE...DEEP BLUE...The color of the ocean. Without water all life withers and dies. Likewise, without **OBEDIENCE**, our Spiritual Life withers and dies. We must be ready to **submit** out wills to the Lord and say *Your will be done* if we wish to feed our Spiritual Life and keep it alive. **OBEDIENCE** is, oddly enough, a **Key to Freedom.**

THE KEY OF LOVE...RED...The heart is the center of the body bringing life-giving nutrients to all the parts of the body. Without it the body cannot function. So, **LOVE** is the heart of the spiritual body: the Body of Christ. **LOVE** calls us to forget ourselves and give freely, using all the gifts that we have been given. Thus the **Body of Christ** becomes a life-giving organism throughout the world.

THE JOURNEY

God has a plan and purpose for each of us. Our journeys are our own. He wants us all to be conformed to the likeness of His Son, Jesus, and He only knows how to accomplish this in each one of us.

Everything that we experience – all that we learn; all the good things; troubles; traumas, etc. are used by our Almighty and Loving God to do just that – form us into the likeness of His Son!

This I believe with all my heart and soul.

And we know that in all things God works for the good of those who love him, who have been called according to his purpose. **Romans 8:28**

God, in His most merciful, loving-kindness turns ALL to our ultimate good!

It is here, my fellow followers of Christ, where the work is. In this **BOOT CAMP** of life and all of its happenings is where we are called to use **THE KEYS TO FREEDOM** to help us become more and more like our precious Savior!

In the coming weeks, we will enter this **BOOT CAMP** together and work through all of our "stuff," so that we may fulfill our destiny to grow like Christ.

PRAYER ASSIGNMENT FOR WEEK 24:

With God's Grace, decide to enter into the **BOOT CAMP**.

Take a deep breath! Rest. Look at how far you've come! You are at the sixth month mark - half the way there.

*But we hold this treasure in earthen vessels that the surpassing power may be of God and not from us. We are afflicted in every way, but not constrained; perplexed, but not driven to despair; persecuted, but not abandoned; struck down, but not destroyed; always carrying about in the body the dying of Jesus, so that the life of Jesus may also be manifested in our body. **2 Corinthians 4:7-10***

THE JOURNEY CAN BE HARD

The apostle Paul experienced many trials along his journey as we read in his letter to the Corinthians, but the negative never prevails. He always has some experience of rescue or salvation!

Paul uses his **KEYS to FREEDOM!** All of us are on our own unique journey and experience heart ache, disappointment, hardship, trauma, and troubles of all kinds. We *are* afflicted in every way!

TIIE BOOT CAMP

I am sure that Paul (along with the other apostles, martyrs throughout the ages and all those on this planet who have faith in God) experienced much WORK to get them through their life's journey.

I call this work the **BOOT CAMP** FOR THE KINGDOM OF GOD! Here we must *Renew Our Minds in Christ...Put On Love.*

These are ACTION words. And action takes PRACTICE and PERSEVERANCE if we are to accomplish such a task! This is where your **KEYS to FREEDOM** come into play.

PERSONAL EXPERIENCE

Some years ago I found myself in a very scary position.

I was out of a job, and the last of my four children was still living at home with me. One day I found this note on my door *NOTIFICATION: THIS PROPERTY MUST BE VACATED WITHIN 24 HOURS.*

The bank had taken possession of the house, and we needed to move. I couldn't pass an application for an apartment because at that time I was without income. I was not able to pay first month's rent, last month's rent or security. And I needed to make sure that I lived in a safe neighborhood because I still had a teenager at home.

What a dilemma! There was no family around to move in with. My first reaction was to call everyone I knew to see if there was somewhere for us to live. Then I went into my prayer spot...curled up...cried and shook with fear!

I then began to speak to the Lord: *I know You love me. I believe You when You said You would provide for me. You are the Good Shepherd, and the Shepherd takes care of His sheep. You say in Your Word that You are a very present help in times of trouble. I am in trouble...You say that I should praise and thank You in all situations...I praise You, and I thank You for giving me a place to live and for providing for me...*

I used my KEYS to work through all of my feelings. I decided to submit to God and remember His promises – to believe, trust and be obedient to His word!

(Trust me, this was not easy...this took work!)

I fell asleep repeating my words of faith.

GOD ANSWERS

I woke up the next morning with a driving sense to call one of my friends. I wasn't sure why I was calling her, but after sharing my dilemma she told me of a place that her sister owned. But she didn't know if it was available.

I phoned her sister, and she told me that the renters had moved out recently and that it was now available! I went to see it. As soon as I turned the corner and saw the house, I knew this was going to be the place for us.

It turned out that this **sense** was God leading and providing for me, and His provision for me was so much more than I could ever imagine. I did not need to pass an application because I knew her sister. A ministry that I had worked with gave me the down payment with enough left over to allow me time to find work before the next rent was due.

To top it all off, she handed me the key and said I could move in at any time.

A church that I had done some volunteer work for had a ministry that helped women in my situation. They set up the water, electric and provided a truck with moving men!

THIS WAS AN ACT OF LOVE.

This reminds me of a song: *He's an on-time God, yes HE is. He may not come when you want Him but He'll be there right on time. He's an on-time God. Yes He is!*

PRAYER ASSIGNMENT FOR WEEK 25: "BOOT CAMP WORKOUT"

Think of a situation in your life that is causing worry or fear. Practice using your **faith, trust, obedience and love keys.**

Hint: Don't ignore your feelings. Practice looking *up* and not *around*! *Pray, Ponder, Journal.*

WEEK 26

LIFE: THE BOOT CAMP

I've been talking to you about using your **KEYS TO FREEDOM** as **SPIRITUAL EXERCISES** in life as a BOOT CAMP. The "happenings" in our lives are there for God to allow us to grow in His likeness. Happenings, like the loss of a job or home can teach us to let go of the many "things" that give us a false sense of security or identity.

We can then use our keys of **FAITH AND TRUST** to help us believe that God is with us and we will be taken care of. If we come into a situation where we have been betrayed or rejected by another, we can use our **OBEDIENCE** key to go to the Word and see what God tells us to do in those situations. Ultimately we will use our **LOVE** key because love is the life-blood of living in THE KINGDOM.

HIDDEN TRUTHS

Many times we are walking through our lives still carrying and reacting from past hurts, disappointments, and traumas. We are afraid to look at these truths - let alone, talk about them - for fear that they will somehow crush us once again. We hide the shame of the experience thinking it will go away. *NOT!!*

What we keep hidden can *still* harm us. I believe this area is the hardest to overcome because these are hidden truths that are in the dark.

Contemplate this Scripture verse:

Then you will know the truth, and the truth will set you free.
John 8:32

BEING SET FREE

A man came to me for prayer. Years ago he lost a son and was still experiencing depression, guilt and regret. He had been living under this "darkness" for many years as it had affected so many areas of his life.

He was afraid to go back to that memory and bring to light what may be causing these deep feelings. As God would have it, he agreed to allow me to pray for him about this most painful dark area in his life.

During the prayer time, it was revealed that his son had broken his leg nine months prior, and it had caused a rare form of bone cancer. This one night he had gotten so bad that the father picked him up and drove him to the hospital emergency room.

He carried his son into the hospital. Then the father remembered that he had left his car running in the front of the emergency entrance, so he went out to park the car. When he returned, his 10 year old son had passed away.

We can only imagine the heartache this man had been enduring all these years - the "secret" that he had hidden deep within his soul. This father had carried so much guilt and regret because he didn't have a chance to say good-bye...that he was not there for his son in those last moments.

Indeed, Jesus was there with him at that time, but because of his trauma at the sudden loss of his son he wasn't able to see Him there.

During this prayer time, our good and loving God gave him the grace to believe...to have **TRUST** and **FAITH** to go back to this memory.

He was given the grace to see Jesus standing at his son's bedside.

He was able to say good-bye to his precious son and tell him how much he loved him.

He was then filled with release... **FREEDOM.**

He had peace for the first time in years! He brought to the **light** what was in the **darkness**.

PRAYER ASSIGNMENT FOR WEEK 26:

Invite the Holy Spirit to come into your subconscious and bring you healing.

EQUIPMENT

There is exercise equipment needed to help develop your Spiritual body when doing your Spiritual Exercises in the **BOOT CAMP.** One piece of that equipment is the **BIBLE – the Guidebook.** For you to *train* in Boot Camp for the Kingdom, you **need** this guide.

There are other pieces of equipment that are available to help you *train;* one being a **CONCORDANCE.** This is a very useful tool for studying the Scriptures. It takes every single word in the Bible and lists where each word can be found. It is useful for locating Scripture verses that you know the words to but not the book, chapter or verse. I recommend *Strong's Concordance* by James Strong.

Another piece of helpful equipment is called a **CYCLOPEDIC INDEX.** This is an awesome tool when doing a study on any subject because it gives a concise definition and includes Scriptures that coincide with the topic. Some Bibles already include a cyclopedic index but if yours doesn't… not to worry… you may purchase this as well as a concordance on *Amazon.com.*

If you don't own either of these helpful tools or pieces of equipment, I suggest you get one or all of them. They are affordable and well worth every cent!

USING THE EQUIPMENT

Daily reading of the Bible is essential to our spiritual growth. If we are dedicated to following Jesus, we *need* to read and contemplate His Word!

I love to read the Psalms. To me they are all about the human condition. In the Psalms I find much comfort, strength, guidance, council and just about anything I need while experiencing my life's journey!

Along with my **BIBLE,** I have found the **CONCORDANCE** and **CYCLOPEDIC INDEX** to be precious pieces of equipment that have aided me in seeking out God's will.

FEAR EXAMPLE

When experiencing FEAR, I look up the word FEAR in the CYCLOPEDIC INDEX of one of my Bibles:

FEAR: anxiety caused by approaching danger 16

Causes:

> Disobedience...*Gen. 3:10*
> Impending judgment...*Heb. 11:7*
> Persecution...*John 20:19*
> Events of nature...*Acts 27: 17, 29*
> Suspicion...*Acts 9: 26*
> Uncertainty...*2 Cor. 11:3*
> Final Events... *Luke 21:26*
> Death...*Heb. 2:15* [16]

Then I am able to ask God to speak to my heart and teach me what I need to learn on this subject.
This becomes a study while learning... listening... growing... healing with my Lord!
I enter the **BOOT CAMP;** I do the **WORK**... the **EXERCISES**... and use the **EQUIPMENT!**
AMEN!

ASSIGNMENT FOR WEEK 27:

Secure your EQUIPMENT!!!

BECOME LIKE CHRIST

You were taught to put off your old self, which belongs to your former manner of life and is corrupt through deceitful desires, and to **be renewed** *in the spirit of your mind and to put on the new self, created after the likeness of God in true righteousness and holiness.* **Ephesians 4:22-24**

To **become,** to be **renewed** means to *grow* (in this case) like Jesus. This takes time, work and perseverance.

Remember the BOOT CAMP. Our lives and our unique journeys are all about Spiritual Growth. It's about becoming like Jesus! Everything that happens to us is used for our GOOD.

God promises, *All things work together for good to those who love God.* **Romans 8:28**

THE BOOT CAMP

Life, our journey, the "happenings" and the way we **act, react and work** through them becomes this **BOOT CAMP**: the **training** ground.

We have tools to use: the Bible, a Concordance, a Cyclopedic Index, and the Keys of Faith, Trust Obedience and Love. We use our wills to surrender to God's ways. We have the Holy Spirit as Helper. How can we fail?

Greater is He that is in you than he that is in the world. **1 John 4:4**

THE PURPOSE

My Sisters and Brothers, fellow followers of Christ, the purpose of this life is to become like Christ (to become holy).

WORK IT

I challenge you to turn all the "stuff" in your life into praise and thanksgiving! I know that long suffering, tragedies and losses are hard. The last thing you want to do is THANK God for them, however, tell God how you feel. Let Him know all of your heartaches and fears. Trust Him to be merciful enough to bear your burdens.

You are human and are allowed to *feel.*

BUT at the end of all that say: *Lord, I will myself to praise and thank You for this because I LOVE You and TRUST You. I have FAITH in You and I know You love me and will use all of this for my good!*

God will bless this act of OBEDIENCE, I promise you! Then get out your BIBLE, CONCORDANCE or CYCLOPEDIC INDEX and start looking up all those words you said to the Lord: fear, anger, heartache. Then listen to what God says to you. Be strengthened and healed by His words!

ASSIGNMENT FOR WEEK 28:

Work it!

How are you doing? Look back...take inventory. In spite of
what you are or are not seeing...

Keep Going!

PREPARING FOR THE BATTLE & THE ARMOR OF GOD

Along with our four keys and our spiritual tools like the Bible, Concordance and Cyclopedic Index, we must also cover ourselves with the **ARMOR OF GOD** just as any warrior would in preparing for a battle because, my Sisters and Brothers, we are in a battle!

Once we decide to follow and obey God, watch out! The devil is going to try every way he can to try and put a stop to it. Remember that the devil knows our weaknesses and all that we have experienced in our lives. You can be sure that he will use any and all of it against us!

However, be of good cheer! We have the **VICTORY IN CHRIST**! We have already won through Him. We have only to keep our eyes LOOKING UP and NOT AROUND! Take a look at what the apostle Paul says about the battle.

Finally, be strong in the Lord and in his mighty power. Put on the full armor of God, so that you can take your stand against the devil's schemes. For our struggle is not against flesh and blood, but against the rulers, against the authorities, against the powers of this dark world and against the spiritual forces of evil in the heavenly realms. Therefore put on the full armor of God, so that when the day of evil comes, you may be able to stand your ground, and after you have done everything, to stand. Stand firm then, with the belt of truth buckled around your waist, with the breastplate of righteousness in place, and with your feet fitted with the readiness that comes from the gospel of peace. In addition to all this, take up the shield of faith, with which you can extinguish all the flaming arrows of the evil one. Take the helmet of salvation and the sword of the Spirit, which is the word of God.
Ephesians 6:10-17

EXAMPLE

A man who is a music minister together with his wife once shared that after the birth of their third child, it was revealed that his wife had been having an affair and had moved in with a man of their church's ministry.

Devastated, he went to his Pastor and confided in him. The sad news is that the pastor did nothing and allowed the wife to continue to minister in the church. I met with him many times and we prayed for the grace to forgive her. He loves Jesus and had made a decision long ago to live his life by God's standards - not the world's.

I soon learned that when he was five years old his mother had abandoned the family, and he never saw or heard from her again.

Now can you imagine the spiritual battle this man was under?

I can just hear Satan's lies: *Oh, this is great... I've got him now... he'll never step foot in church again! He will never forgive her. After all, he can't face that deep sorrow of his mom leaving...let alone his wife...oh, it is just too much for him. Maybe I can even get him to give up all together! Another one LOST forever with me!*

NOT AND NO! You see, this man knows Jesus. He knows that the victory is already won.

He used his Faith, Trust, Obedience and Love Keys. He stayed in Scripture, prayed and put on that **Armor** every day. And he got through it!

It took time, but with God's help and love, this man stood firm and worked through it with God's grace. He experienced much healing even as deep as that sorrow of his mom leaving!

What Satan means for *evil*, God means for *good.* Praise God!

PRAYER ASSIGNMENT FOR WEEK 29:

Keep praying; keep doing the work. Now put on the ARMOR!

DEATH

Although physical death is inevitable for all of us, when we are faced with it our world can be shattered. Let's face it - even though death is a part of life, it can throw us for a loop, especially if it is tragic or unexpected. Our worlds are forever changed.

There are many different reactions when faced with death. Some of us go into a deep depression or anger that can take years to uncover, and all the while the devil has his way into our lives.

You see, we can't go about our lives with hidden truths because they take energy to suppress and when that "nerve" to the secret is touched - watch out!

I remember when my siblings and I lost our dad in a tragic boating accident. It was like an atomic bomb went off in our lives, sending all of us out in different directions. It was years later when we were together again and able to talk about what happened.

Brothers and Sisters: we know that if our earthly dwelling, a tent, should be destroyed, we have a building from God, a dwelling not made with hands, eternal in heaven. **2 Corinthians 5:1**

I think of a veil that separates us from those who are in heaven. They are still all around us, but behind the veil. As we ask Mother Mary and all the saints who have gone before us to pray for us, now we can ask our loved ones and friends to pray for us. After all, they now know the truth, understand it all, and know us. Their prayers for us are powerful.

The most awesome thing that we have to look forward to is that WE WILL BE REUNITED ONCE AGAIN!

Do not let your hearts be troubled. Trust in God; trust also in me. In my Father's house are many rooms; if it were not so, I would have told you. I am going there to prepare a place for you. And if I go and prepare a place for you, I will come back and take you to be with me that you also may be where I am. You know the way to the place where I am going. **John 14:1-4**

ACT

Remember that we are all on our own unique journeys. All of our "happenings" are opportunities for us to grow in holiness and become more like Jesus. When facing death, it is important to do the following: give yourself time to grieve; be patient with yourself; lean on your FAITH and TRUST keys; pray; and read God's Word.

When you feel a little better, look up death in your Cyclopedic Index and Concordance and listen to your Lord.

Put on the Armor of God so that the devil will not take advantage of this difficult time in your life. Look up and not around. God's grace and love will carry you through!

PRAYER ASSIGNMENT FOR WEEK 30:

Ask Jesus to go with you into your death experience. See Him there...

Remember to follow the steps on page 3.

Brothers and Sisters, we are called to **PRAISE** and **WORSHIP** our God.

PRAISE: According to Dictionary.com the definition of **Praise** is act of expressing approval or admiration; commendation; laudation: the offering of grateful homage in words or song, as an act of worship: a hymn of praise to God: to offer grateful homage to (God or a deity), as in words or song.

Praise the Lord with harp: sing unto him with the psaltery and an instrument of ten strings. **Psalm 33:2**

By him therefore let us offer the sacrifice of praise to God continually, this is, the fruit of our lips, giving thanks to His name. **Hebrews 13:15**

Sing praise to the LORD, you His godly ones, and give thanks to His holy name... **Psalm 30:4**

WORSHIP: The Merriam-Webster online dictionary defines Worship as the feeling or expression of reverence and adoration for a deity: "ancestor worship". If used as a verb: Show reverence and adoration for (a deity); honor with religious rites.

Give unto the Lord the glory due unto his name: bring an offering, and come before him: worship the Lord our maker. **1 Chronicles 16:29**

O come, let us worship and bow down: let us kneel before the Lord our maker. **Psalm 95:6**

O worship the Lord in the beauty of holiness: fear before him, all the earth. **Psalm 96:9**

These scriptures are a very small example of the many more found in the Bible!

BENEFITS OF PRAISE AND WORSHIP

When you **Praise** and **Worship** God, you are bringing down His **presence** because **He inhabits** the praises of His people. *Psalm 100:4*

When you praise and worship God, He manifests His **power**. *Acts 16:30-31*

HIS POWER SAVES, HEALS AND DELIVERS.

When you praise and worship God, the **glory of God** comes down. *1 Kings 8:10-11*

When you praise and worship God, the **anointing** of God descends upon His servants. Because of this they are able to minister more effectively. *II Kings 3:15-16*

When you praise and worship God, the **deliverance power** of God comes into play. *II Chronicles 20:1-20*

God comes down to deliver His people as they praise and worship Him.

PRAYER ASSIGNMENT FOR WEEK 31:

Look in your BIBLE for Scriptures on PRAISE and WORSHIP. Use your CYCLOPEDIC INDEX and/or your CONCORDANCE to help with this study. Then PRAISE and WORSHIP God in your prayer time, and if you have the opportunity to attend a PRAISE and WORSHIP service and/ or prayer group...do so! *Keep up your prayer and journaling.*

Just to review:

Spiritual exercises are like being in **BOOT CAMP**! Our commanding officer is God; we need to obey His commands!

How will we know what His commands are if we aren't listening to His words and then practicing to act on them?

We need to cultivate a personal relationship with our Father in heaven. This takes time - time to both talk and time to listen...time to share our lives, our hopes, dreams, joys, hurts, etc. In our spiritual lives, this is called **PRAYER**.

PRAYER is the essence of the spiritual exercise we need to commit to on a regular basis! Think of it as though you are in boot camp for the armed service. You will need to be physically fit for your military task ahead, so you must be spiritually fit for your life's journey - your task here on earth!

MY PRAYER TIME

For my prayer time, I find a quiet, uninterrupted time and place. I rest in a comfortable position and ask the Holy Spirit to fall fresh on me, guide me, and give me wisdom and discernment.

Then I like to:

Enter His gates with thanksgiving and His courts with praise. **Psalm 100:4**

As I begin my prayer, I picture walking into the throne room to approach the Almighty! I move into praising Him. I might sing songs to my Lord or recite the praise Psalms. Then I begin thanking Him for **ALL** that is going on in my life.

Remember we changed *asking* God to *thanking* God.

I find that by thanking God I receive much grace. I believe it enables God to act freely in me because of my surrender!

As I surrender to His will, I listen...sit quietly...read Scripture...use my Concordance to look up words that describe my feelings about what is happening in my life. And I continue listening. The rest of the prayer time is determined by what the Holy Spirit does. By that I mean I receive **"discernment."** For example: Maybe I become aware of a memory that needs healing, or I am made aware of a person I need to forgive. Maybe the Holy Spirit is instructing me to learn something and so on. When I receive the **"discernment,"** I am able to respond as I would to anyone who had just spoken to me.

My prayer time then becomes a conversation or communion with My Lord! I end with thanking and praising God once again, and I say things like *The glory is all yours, Lord!*

I also like to keep a journal about the discernments I have received. I find this practice invaluable. As I go through my journey, I sometimes experience doubt, confusion, lack of faith or trust, and with my journals I am able to look back over my entries and see the movements of God in my life.

I am then able to remember how He has been there for me – how He's healed, taught, inspired, comforted and strengthened me!

The Scripture says: I remember the days of old; I meditate on all Your doings; I muse on the work of Your hands. ***Psalm 143:5***

SOME ADVANTAGES OF PRAYER:

1. It will draw you closer to God.
2. It will remind you of who God is and what He has done for you.
3. It will help you to grow in love for God and His word.
4. It will help you to experience the love of God.
5. It will be a source of comfort and strength.
6. It will give you discernments and spiritual growth.
7. It will change you in unexpected ways.[17]

PRAYER ASSIGNMENT FOR WEEK 32:

Experiment with some of the ways I've shared with you about my prayer time!

Rest. You are doing great work...

Do you feel those spiritual muscles?

BACKSLIDING

Backsliding, also known as **falling away** is a term used within Christianity to describe a process by which an individual who has converted to Christianity *reverts to pre-conversion habits and/or lapses or falls into sin, when a person turns from God to pursue their own desire.*[18]

I have experienced **backsliding** more times than I care to admit. I have experienced doubt, lack of trust and fear. I have reverted to old habits, falling into sinful attitudes and doing my own thing.

Unfortunately those times were some of the darkest in my life; conversely those times have brought me to a deeper maturity in my spiritual life.

My brethren, count it all joy when you fall into various trials, knowing that the testing of your faith produces patience. But let patience have its perfect work, that you may be perfect and complete, lacking nothing. **James 1:2-3**

And we know that all things work together for good to them that love God, to them who are the called according to his purpose. **Romans 8:28**

THE "ENEMY"

When we decide to follow God, you better believe that the **enemy** is out to stop us in any way possible. St. Ignatius of Loyola is the author of **THE DISCERNMENT OF SPIRITS** in which he says that there are two kinds of spirits, good and bad.

The bad he calls the **enemy.** If we are not aware, understand, or reject the **enemy** we will be distanced from God and His plan for our lives.

This **enemy** consists of: (1) the *adversary 1 Peter 5:8*...the *tempter Matthew 4:3*...the *liar and father of lies John 8:44*. This **enemy** comes from **outside** of us or (2) our own redeemed but fragile humanity: the apostle Paul calls it *the flesh and it has desires against the Spirit. Galatians 5:17*. This includes all of our history; our wounds; hurts; self-doubts; fear and burdens.

This **enemy** comes from **within** us, but (3) another **enemy** comes from **around** us, and it is the world...society...culture. Though our world is a gift from God and is filled with many wonders we must remember that *we are not of this world. John 17:14-16*

These enemies will cause us to **BACKSLIDE** or **FALL AWAY** from God and miss the many blessings He has for us on our life's journey.

THE GOOD NEWS

The good news is that we have the victory in our faith in God. Jesus has already won!

But thanks be to God! He gives us the victory through our Lord Jesus Christ. 1 Corinthians 15:57

In this world you will have trouble. But take heart! I have overcome the world. John 16:33

Brothers and Sisters do not be discouraged. We are all human beings and fall away through sin - disappointing ourselves, one another and most of all, our Father in heaven.

The good news is that we are forgiven... loved... redeemed... helped... healed!

PRAYER ASSIGNMENT FOR WEEK 33:

Identify your **enemies** with the help of the Holy Spirit. Then get into the BOOT CAMP using the KEYS to FREEDOM – PRAYER, your BIBLE, CYCLOPEDIC INDEX, and CONCORDANCE to work through to VICTORY! *Journal... remember to look back each week.*

FINANCIAL CHALLENGES

I meet, talk and pray with many people each day who are experiencing much anxiety, fear, worry, anger, bitterness, and depression over financial challenges. So many of us have lost or are in the process of losing our homes, jobs, savings, and our investments – things we've worked hard for over many years.

I have prayed with people who are suffering over the loss of their family due to these financial losses. People may also lose their health; suffering from heart attacks... strokes... ulcers... diseases... cancer... the list goes on!

But the most heartbreaking scenario is when someone is left to pick up the pieces after their loved one took their own life *as a result* of financial pressures.

THE GOOD SHEPHERD

I AM THE GOOD SHEPHERD... **JOHN 10:14**

While on a retreat some years ago I listened while the speaker talked about her growing up in Switzerland in a small farm town. In this town many of the people owned sheep, and she shared some facts about sheep and their shepherds.

She said that sheep are not very smart and can be **easily led** away from the flock and **get lost**. At the end of each day, the shepherd counts his sheep. And if there is one lost he must go and find it – sometimes climbing steep mountains into the dark night in search of the lost one.

The shepherd actually **risks his life** to find the lost sheep and bring it back to the flock!

Another interesting fact is that if a sheep falls over, as they often do, they are not able to get up by themselves; therefore, the shepherd is responsible for going out to find the sheep who have fallen over and **rescue** them from the danger of wolves! The shepherd is **responsible** and **dedicated** to the total care of his sheep - he feeds, protects, and guides them.

A couple of more facts: *Each shepherd has his own distinct call and the sheep know that call and respond to it. And each sheep will rub up against the shepherd one time a day!*

REMEMBER THE BOOT CAMP

Brothers and Sisters, if you are experiencing financial challenges, please hear this:

JESUS is your **PROVIDER, PROTECTOR and GUIDE.** He gave his life for you. He loves you. He will never leave you! The Lord is **RESPONSIBLE** and **DEDICATED** to you. **HE *IS* THE GOOD SHEPHERD!**

If you haven't been training in the **Boot Camp** now is the time to get to it. Make the decision to use your **FAITH** and **TRUST KEYS**. Read your **BIBLE**. Use the **CYCLOPEDIC INDEX** and **CONCORDANCE**. Set time to **PRAY;** *RUB UP AGAINST YOUR LORD EACH DAY...*

Be thankful that your Lord is taking care of you and guiding you through this trial. Ask the Holy Spirit to reveal to you the root of your fear, worry, and anxiety.

And remember, *ALL THINGS WORK TOGETHER FOR GOOD.* **Romans 8:28**

THE REASON

My brethren, count it all joy when you fall into various trials knowing that the testing of your faith produces patience but let patience have its perfect work, that you may be perfect and complete, lacking nothing... **James 1:1-4**

Know that God is allowing this in your life at this time. And it is for your ultimate GOOD!

PRAYER ASSIGNMENT FOR WEEK 34:

If you are under financial challenges, work in the "Boot Camp." If you know someone who is going through this remind them of THE GOOD SHEPHERD!

WE CAN'T FIGURE GOD OUT

Are you one of those people who study... strive... even are obsessed with trying to figure God out? You might read all spiritual books... join every bible study...attend every conference... even go to self- help groups...eager to try every means possible to try and figure God out.   Even more to the point: what and why is God doing or not doing in your life and in the world? I was one of those people! Thank God I took time to pray and study the scriptures:

Then I saw all the work of God, that man cannot find out the work that is done under the sun. However much man may toil in seeking, he will not find it out. Even though a wise man claims to know, he cannot find it out. **Ecclesiastes 8:17**

Our God is the CREATOR OF THE UNIVERSE!

There are over 900 names and titles for God in Scripture – each describing another aspect of God.

Here are just a few: **ALPHA AND OMEGA, ANOINTED ONE, AUTHOR OF LIFE, A VERY PRESENT HELP IN TIMES OF TROUBLE, BREAD OF LIFE, BAPTIZER, CHIEF SHEPHERD, JESUS, CHRIST THE KING, COMFORTER, COUNSELOR, CREATOR OF HEAVENS AND EARTH, DELIVERER, EVERLASTING GOD, ETERNAL LIFE, FATHER, HOLY ONE, HOLY SPIRIT, I AM, SAVIOR, LIGHT, LIVING STONE, MIGHTY, OUR PEACE, REFUGE, and the list goes on and on!**

How could we ever comprehend *anything* of this God and why He does or doesn't do wondrous works...and yet...we must still try!

I GOT FOOLED

My son underwent three experimental heart surgeries and was still dying. There seemed to be no help anywhere for repairing his rare heart defects.

Then the Good Lord miraculously allowed us to "stumble" upon a surgeon who might be able to help us, our doctors thought. After a heart catheterization in Alabama Hospital the doctor came into our room to give us the news.

He sat down across from me and ever so gently said, "Your son is dying, and if I put him through surgery *now* he will never live through it. If he were my son I would take him home and enjoy every moment with him. If he has another attack and lives through it, come back and I will try something in surgery."

Well, you would think with that news I would be hysterical, but as he spoke it was as if a healing balm came from him and flowed over me. I knew God was with me as I received a great grace of peace.

I knew this was the right answer.

After nine months he did have another attack. We were able to return to that hospital, and the same doctor was able to complete the surgery. He said he gave him more time. A few years later we were back in the hospital in Alabama. This time we sat around a large table with the whole team of doctors.

We were told that our son was going to die. No estimate on how long he had and no guarantees that he would survive surgery.

I was confident that God would speak through that same surgeon and that I would, once again, receive that some grace - that healing balm – that had come over me before.

Except this time, no grace...no healing balm! I then realized that I thought I had figured God out.

"For My thoughts are not your thoughts, nor are your ways My ways," says the Lord. "For as the heavens are higher than the earth, so are My ways higher than your ways, and My thoughts than your thoughts. **Isaiah 55:8-9**

My son survived.

PRAYER ASSIGNMENT FOR WEEK 35:

Consider where/why you are trying to figure God out! *By now you should be in the habit of praying, pondering and journaling.*

LET'S TALK MIRACLES

Throughout the Old and New Testament there are many accounts of miracles.

Here are just a few.

Moses sees a burning bush and God speaks to him; *Exodus 3:1-10*. The sun stood still; *Joshua 10:12-13*. An angel defeats thousands; *2 Kings 19:35-36*. Jesus heals a crippled hand; *Mark 3:3-5*. Jesus is transfigured; *Luke 9:28-36*. Peter escapes from prison; *Acts 12*.

Likewise, throughout the centuries, miracles have taken place in many parts of the world, and sometimes in our own backyards!

Our own beautiful Blessed Mother appeared at Lourdes in France, Fatima in Portugal, and Medjugorje in Bosnia.

Let's not forget all of the Eucharistic miracles that have taken place all over the world over the centuries.

In Siena, Italy the Consecrated Host remained perfectly preserved for over 250 years; The Eucharist was thrown into a fire overnight and was miraculously untouched in Amsterdam, Holland; and the unbelieving Priests of Bolsena-Orviet and Lanciano, Italy witnessed the Consecrated Host turn to flesh and blood![19]

SOUL MIRACLES

To me, **CONVERSIONS,** or what I call **SOUL MIRACLES,** are the most awesome testament to God's amazing power. There is no person alive that could touch a person's soul and heart and *change* it the way our Lord can.

Think about St. Paul. He went from killing and persecuting Christians to becoming one. St. Francis was a rich indulgent. St. Ignatius was a military warrior.

123

Many of our contemporaries have also experienced a **SOUL MIRACLE.**

One such person is the one-time New York gang member Nicky Cruz whose life was miraculously transformed by our Lord. I am sure you have been a witness to seeing people's lives make miraculous changes once they encounter God.

Their hearts have been changed to the point that you can see it by their words and deeds. Sometimes these **SOUL MIRACLES** happen over time, and sometimes they are immediate! To me, the most precious of these miracles are the ones that take place during the **HEALING MEMORIES** prayer.

HEALING MEMORIES

Jesus is the same yesterday, today and tomorrow. There is no time constriction with God. For this reason we are able to go back to a particular memory or a traumatic event that took place in our past and invite Jesus to be with us in that memory and heal it. After all, Jesus was there with us when it happened!

And behold, I am with you always, to the end of the age.
Matthew 28:20

These are some precious **SOUL MIRACLES** that I have been privileged to witness during healing prayer: a person forgiving their abuser and receiving peace for the first time in years; someone recognizing their own guilt and receiving the grace to forgive themselves; one being able to let go of the child they had lost; someone coming to terms with an injustice put upon them; and the most precious of all is when a person is able to receive God's love when they are finally convinced that they are a worthwhile person!

PRAYER ASSIGNMENT FOR WEEK 36:

Consider all of the miracles that the good Lord has allowed you to see. Meditate on how each one has influenced you along your life.

Rest and look at all you've come through thus far!

HEALING MEMORIES & SOUL MIRACLES cont.

Along our journeys we will most likely experience some *healing of memories* or **Soul Miracles.**

Jesus said:

*The Spirit of the Lord is upon me, because he has anointed me to proclaim good news to the poor. He has sent me to proclaim freedom for the prisoners and recovery of sight for the blind, to set the oppressed free. **Luke 4:18***

It is so oppressive, even tortuous, to live as an emotional prisoner because of past guilt, hurt, trauma or disappointment. These "happenings" have the potential to scar us to the point where it holds us back from becoming the people God intends us to be and receive the many blessings He has for us!

These scars may cause us to react with harsh words, hateful thoughts - even violent behaviors. We project our past into the present, and many innocent beings get hurt as a result. We are often **blinded** to this fact.

But Jesus said:

*Come to me, all you who are weary and burdened, and I will give you rest. **Matthew 11:28***

EXAMPLE

Lois came to me for healing prayer.

She was a beautiful woman who loved Jesus and had been a faithful and obedient follower. She understood the ways of The Kingdom. Lois was having difficulty with one of her coworkers - a **Latina-woman** named Angelina.

It seemed that every time Angelina was anywhere near her, Lois would experience anxiety and hateful thoughts towards her. Lois was obedient to Jesus' command to *Pray for your enemies. **Matthew 5:44,*** but these feelings persisted.

This antipathy escalated so much that Lois considered not even going into work for fear that she would run into Angelina!

We then began praying, asking for the Holy Spirit for wisdom and discernment. As the prayer continued the Lord revealed a traumatic memory that had been hidden deep into Lois' memory.

Many years ago Lois experienced an emotional breakdown and was placed in a hospital. She was restrained to her bed and given medication by injection. It so happened that the person who came in to give these injections was a **Latina woman!**

The Lord, in His most precious mercy and love, brought Lois through this memory. She was able to speak forgiveness to this woman and come to terms with what was part of who she was – a beautiful daughter of God who suffered from bi-polar disorder.

Jesus had set her free. He gave her sight! Lois had a **SOUL MIRACLE...** *a beautiful healing of a memory.*

Incidentally... did you realize that *Angel*ina was a **GIFT** to Lois?

*And we know that for those who love God, all things work together for good, for those who are called according to his purpose. **Romans 8:28***

PRAYER ASSIGNMENT FOR WEEK 37:

Contemplate things in your life that cause you anxiety, fear, or stress. Praise and thank God for these GIFTS; allow the Lord to give you new sight and freedom. Experience a **Soul Miracle**. *Please journal these.*

THE BATTLE & REINFORCEMENT

I have shared the Boot Camp for the Kingdom with you.

I have advised about preparing for battle.

If you want to follow Jesus then you are in a battle – the world against the Kingdom of God.

No one can serve two masters. Either you will hate the one and love the other, or you will be devoted to the one and despise the other. You cannot serve both God and money (the world). **Luke 16:13**

We have worked on improving our **spiritual muscles** to prepare and work through the battle by putting on the *Armor of God* (*Ephesians 6:10-17*) by using the **Tools,** such as the **Keys to Freedom – Faith, Trust, Obedience** and **Love – the Bible, Concordance and Cyclopedic Index...** and of course **Prayer.**

We also have many **reinforcements** available for our use.

Today I will focus on some excellent books of reinforcement that help in this battle for **THE KINGDOM:**

JESUS CALLING Enjoying Peace In His Presence by **Sarah Young** is a daily devotional that I treasure. Sarah is a missionary who kept a prayer journal for years. She decided to spend time in meditation, listening to what the Lord had to say to her. These inspirations evolved into this devotional! I like to read it in the morning and contemplate it during the day. I find it amazing that her words often reflect the very thing God is speaking to me about that day.

GOD CALLING by **A.J.RUSSELL** is another daily devotional. These meditations confirm God's love to us. This is also great to read in the morning, so that you can keep the words deep in your heart all day!

THE IMITATION OF CHRIST by **Thomas A. Kempis.** WOW! All I can say is that if you really want to be like Jesus - this is a gem. It's a **CLASSIC** work written somewhere between the years 1379-1471. Read one section a day, so that you may contemplate the profound spiritual meaning. I also suggest that you buy it containing a **Spiritual Commentary and Reader's guide**. The one I recommend is by **Dennis Billy, C.Ss.R.** This version also includes the Contemporary Translation by **William C. Creasy.**

ABANDONMENT TO DIVINE PROVIDENCE by **Jean-Pierre De Caussade** and translated by John Beevers is another exemplary devotional. If you want to be assured of *leaving it all to God* - this is for you!

33 DAYS TO MORNING GLORY by **Fr. Michael E. Gaitley, MIC.** The goal of our lives and journey is to become holy. In this book Fr. Gaitley teaches us the surest, quickest and easiest way to achieve that - consecrate yourself to Jesus through **The Blessed Mother Mary**! This book gives the perspectives of **St. Louis de Montford, St. Maximilian Kolbe, Blessed Teresa of Calcutta and Blessed Pope John Paul II** on consecration to **Jesus through Mary.** The book is amazing!

You can purchase all this literature and more on Amazon.com

PRAYER ASSIGNMENT FOR WEEK 38:

Thank God for leading you to a book that will reinforce you on your journey at this time. Then get it!

Remember that our goal is to become **holy** and **spiritually free** – to grow into the persons that God created us to be!

And do not be conformed to this world, but be transformed by the renewing of your mind, in order to prove by you what is that good and pleasing and perfect will of God. **Romans 12:2**

For our struggle is not against flesh and blood, but against the rulers, against the authorities, against the powers of this dark world and against the spiritual forces of evil in the heavenly realms. **Ephesians 6:12**

We are in a battle, but remember that we have many <u>tools</u> available to help us. When we "work it" it is like being in a spiritual exercise program or **BOOT CAMP for the Kingdom**!

MORE REINFORCEMENT

Here are some more reinforcements that have been a great help to me along my journey.

THE LITURGY OF THE HOURS, DIVINE OFFICE OR THE BREVIARY

This book contains primarily Psalms that are supplemented by hymns and readings and meant to be prayed three times a day. This is an ancient practice coming from the Jewish tradition and is prescribed by the Catholic Church to be recited by Clergy, Laity and Religious Institutes.

You may purchase the Liturgy of The Hours on *Amazon.com*. It is published in a three book series; however, I find it very confusing to follow so I take the easy route and go to *divineoffice.org*.

All of the prayers are in order and you can even listen to the audio if you prefer.

I do love praying three times a day by following these prayers. Try it. You may like it!!

BOOKS ABOUT SAINTS

I get so much out of reading about the lives of the Saints.

I especially love the Mystics:

St. Theresa of Avilla, *Interior Castles*; St. John of the Cross, *The Dark Night of the Soul*; St. Padre Pio, *Padre Pio in America*; Blessed Mother Theresa, *Her Diary* and all of her writings! There are tons of books on Saints, and I think they are really insightful.

I receive such deep revelations when I read these great books. I am always amazed at how these faithful people lived out their journey by the revelations they received as they served and loved God. The same Holy Spirit empowered... led... graced... inspired... and gifted them as He does today for *us*!

PRAYER ASSIGNMENT FOR WEEK 39:

Thank God for all the reinforcements He graces you with. Make note of them in your journal through your journey.

FALSE REINFORCEMENTS

Read and contemplate these Scriptures:

Do not be deceived: Evil Company corrupts good habits. **1 Corinthians 15:33**

A perverse man sows strife, and a whisperer separates close friends. **Proverbs 16:28**

Make no friendships with a man given to anger, and with a wrathful man do not associate. **Proverbs 22:24**

One who has unreliable friends soon comes to ruin, but there is a friend who sticks closer than a brother. **Proverbs 18:24**

My Sisters and Brothers,

Evil, Perversity, Secrecy, Anger, Wrath, Undependability, Gossip

These words are descriptive of the *world* not the **Kingdom**. We are *not* of this world, we are in it.

We, the followers of Christ, have decided to follow God's ways and not our own. **We cannot and should not go to friends who are walking in the world for any type of guidance or help.** So many times I hear people say that they confided in a friend who gave them advice, and my question to them is, *do they understand the ways of God and have they made a decision to follow Him?*

If the answer is *no* then they will not be a source for reinforcement to become holy and follow God! I am not saying that you should eliminate your non-believing friends or family.

Simply please do not share your "stuff" with anyone who does not understand the Kingdom and its ways.

TRUE REINFORCEMENTS

Read and contemplate these Scriptures:

But the wisdom from above is first pure, then peaceable, gentle, open to reason, full of mercy and good fruits, impartial and sincere. And a harvest of righteousness is sown in peace by those who make peace. **James 3:17-18**

Blessed is the man who walks not in the counsel of the wicked, nor stands in the way of sinners, nor sits in the seat of scoffers; but his delight is in the law of the Lord, and on his law he meditates day and night. He is like a tree planted by streams of water that yields its fruit in its season, and its leaf does not wither. In all that he does, he prospers. **Psalm 1:1-3**

People in our lives who understand and walk the ways of the Kingdom are great sources of reinforcement for us who are on the journey toward becoming holy.

PRAYER ASSIGNMENT FOR WEEK 40:

Ask the Holy Spirit to reveal truth about who you share with.

You are almost there! Take a break.

THE CRUCIBLE

My friends in Christ, all of us at one time or another will experience being refined. Some call it entering the CRUCIBLE - the fire. God allows us to enter into circumstances - the crucible or fire that will "melt and mold" us into the people God has envisioned for us to become!

Think of gold. It needs to be put into a high heated furnace to be *melted* so that the Artist can *mold* and shape it into its fullest glorious potential. Only the Artist knows what He wants the piece to look like He knows its beauty and purpose.

So it is with Our Father in heaven. He knows what beauty there is within each of us, He knows what purpose He has for each one of us. He lovingly allows us to enter into the crucible to accomplish His will.

THE "ARTIST" KNOWS

Six years ago a man came to me for prayer.

He had been working for a company for twenty years, and the owner assured him that if he would obtain licensure he could then become a partner in that company.

Eager to become a partner, the man set out to his studies. Along the way he had a conversion experience! He began to speak up about some of the illegal practices that he had, in fact, participated in but no longer felt so inclined. He completed his studies and passed the exam for his license. But when he presented it to his boss, he was fired.

The man was filled with anger, a sense of betrayal and fear about how he would support his family. In prayer, we discerned that the Lord was with him and "all would be well." I urged him to pray for his boss and to forgive him. He searched for a job over the next year; lost all three of his houses; all of his cars and most of his family's possessions. All the while, he felt humiliated.

He finally was able to get a job pumping gas at a filling station. He stayed there for five years while the Lord changed his heart. He went through the **CRUCIBLE**!

The man spent many hours praying, listening and looking to God for answers. He entered into the BOOT CAMP! He used his FAITH, TRUST, OBEDIENCE and LOVE KEYS and many REINFORCEMENTS (spiritual books, spiritual direction, the Bible) to work through this time and persevere!

While at work one day he met a man who he had worked with years ago who told him that he and another man had wanted to get in touch with him.

Now these men had worked in the same field that he had gotten his licensure for, and upon reconnecting with them they offered him a job! It wasn't any job. It was to RUN their company!

This man said to me that God had to teach him humility. He not only grew as a man but he grew spiritually, and he would now run this company by God's standards. He is a much better husband and father and soon becoming one of the leaders in his church community!

DID GOD, THE ARTIST, KNOW THE BEAUTY AND PURPOSE THAT HE HAD PLANNED FOR THIS MAN? DID HE LOVINGLY ALLOW HIM TO GO THROUGH THE FIRE...THE CRUCIBLE...TO MELT AND MOLD HIM? **YOU BET HE DID!**

PRAYER ASSIGNMENT FOR WEEK 41:

Look at the crucible you are in. Cooperate with where you are. Thank God for where you are. Allow your loving Father to melt and mold you.

PERSEVERE. Get into BOOT CAMP. ——*Read PSALM 121.*

I once met a wonderful, faith filled woman who knew Mother Theresa.

In one of our conversations she said this to me: *Mother once turned and pointed her finger at me and said, don't you ever think that all these good works you do will get you into heaven. It won't. It is when you can see the face of Jesus in every person that you will enter heaven! This is* **LOVE.**

First Corinthians 13 reads as the following:

If I speak in the tongues of men or of angels, but do not have **love***, I am only a resounding gong or a clanging cymbal. If I have the gift of prophecy and can fathom all mysteries and all knowledge, and if I have a faith that can move mountains but do not have* **love***, I am nothing. If I give all I possess to the poor and give over my body to hardship that I may boast, but do not have* **love***, I gain nothing.*

Love is patient, love is kind. It docs not envy, it does not boast, it is not proud. It does not dishonor others, it is not self-seeking, it is not easily angered, and it keeps no record of wrongs. Love does not delight in evil but rejoices with the truth. It always protects, always trusts, always hopes, and always perseveres. Love never fails.

But where there are prophecies, they will cease; where there are tongues, they will be stilled; where there is knowledge, it will pass away. For we know in part and we prophesy in part, but when completeness comes, what is in part disappears. When I was a child, I talked like a child; I thought like a child, I reasoned like a child. When I became a man, I put the ways of childhood behind me. For now we see only a reflection as in a mirror; then we shall see face to face. Now I know in part; then I shall know *fully, even as I am fully known. And now these three remain: faith, hope and love. But the greatest of these is **love**.*

OUR UNIQUE JOURNEY

The Lord knows what each one of us needs to become holy in our journey to grow to be more like Him. He allows circumstances in our lives to help shape us to that end. As you read the Scripture on what LOVE is, do you find that it describes you and your actions?

I know that the Lord is still working with me on many of these attributes and will continue until I go home to be with Him. Remember, we are on a journey – an ongoing growing, learning and changing experience. We are given opportunities to CHOOSE Christ and His ways at every moment.

Get into the BOOT CAMP and work it!

BOOT CAMP

If you want to strengthen your muscles, you commit to daily exercise. So it is in the BOOT CAMP for the KINGDOM to commit to exercise your Spiritual muscles!

Read Scripture... Pray... Listen... Contemplate... Use your Keys to Freedom: Faith, Trust, Obedience and Love...Use your Concordance and Cyclopedic Index... Receive the Eucharist... Give yourself to the Blessed Mother... Read the lives of the Saints... Ask the Holy Spirit to show you Truth and the root to your actions. Go to Spiritual direction.

PRAYER ASSIGNMENT FOR WEEK 42:

Read and listen to the Scriptures on LOVE with your **heart**. Contemplate them. Thank the Holy Spirit for revealing the truth to you about how you LOVE.

BEING A PHARISEE

Definition of **PHARISEE**: a member of a Jewish sect of the intertestamental period noted for strict observance of rites and ceremonies of the written law and for insistence on the validity of their own oral traditions concerning the law.[20]

This relates to all believers. These are our Sister and Brother Christians – the people we worship God with in our own churches. These folks believe that there are only **correct** ways to worship God. This includes how to sing, pray, read the bible, and essentially be a Christian. They believe these ways are, certainly, the *only* way that things **should** be done! I have been guilty of this myself.

My friends, there are seven things that God considers an abomination:

Haughty eyes, a lying tongue, hands that shed innocent blood, a heart that devises wicked plans, feet that make haste to run to evil, a false witness who breathes out lies, and one who sows discord among brothers. **Proverbs 6:16-19**

I have experienced such "Pharisees" among my Christian Sisters and Brothers throughout the years of my faith walk and throughout my work for the church. Too many times I have met and prayed with those who were deeply hurt and broken, as I have been, by those "Pharisees."

They were judged and rejected by their Sisters and Brothers in Christ for a myriad of reasons, including divorced; immigrants or newcomers; living together before marriage; had an abortion; too liberal; too conservative; not rich enough; gay; too unconventional in their thinking, and the list goes on.

Pastors, too, have been hurt. They have been removed by parishioners (Pharisees) because the pastor came with a vision for the parish that was different than what they were used to.

It is true that some of the Pharisees' "stuff" is rooted from insecurity and fear. They may need power and control to feel better about themselves or to feel safe. Whatever the reason, this strict way of thinking blocks the work of the Holy Spirit in our lives and in the Church. It hurts us. The Pharisees opposed Jesus. But remember, God is **love**. Jesus heals. Jesus forgives. The time has come to stop judging and start loving. *This* heals.

Love the Lord your God with all your heart and with all your soul and with your entire mind. This is the first and most important command. And the second command is like it: Love your neighbor as you love yourself. All the Law and the Prophets hang on these two commandments. **Matthew 22:37-40**

PRAYER ASSIGNMENT FOR WEEK 43:

My Sisters and Brothers, please take time to read and contemplate Proverbs 6:16-19 with your heart.

Ask the Holy Spirit to reveal this to you...Are *you* a Pharisee?

BEING A PHARISEE cont.

Last week your prayer assignment was to ask the Holy Spirit to reveal the truth to you. *Are you or have you ever been a Pharisee?* If you realized that there was some truth for you than I want to remind you that God hates the *sin* but loves the sinner. **He loves you.**

The Spirit of the Sovereign Lord is on me, because the Lord has anointed me to proclaim good news to the poor. He has sent me to bind up the brokenhearted, to proclaim freedom for the captives and release from darkness for the prisoners. **Isaiah 61:1**

When the Lord convicts us of a sin, it is because He wants to help us grow and be set free of our "stuff."

Please remember to use this prayer to help you become free:

1. I renounce the negativity of___, and I take authority over you and command you to be gone out of my life in Jesus' name. 2. Oh Father, I am so sorry for the ways I cooperate with this negativity, whether I know it or not, and I ask for your forgiveness. 3. Thank you, Lord, for your mercy and forgiveness towards me. 4. I now receive all the blessings that you pour out on my life and destiny.

BEING HURT BY A PHARISEE

I am a person who has been hurt many times by my Sisters and Brothers in Christ (Pharisees). I will give one example: Years ago when my baby was going through one heart surgery after another I reached out to any and all prayer groups to pray for my son. It was so beautiful to know that there were prayers being lifted up for him all over the world!

One day after church, a woman asked how my son was doing. After I shared his status with her she said: *The reason your son is not healed is because you don't have enough faith.*

She told me **I WAS NOT HOLY ENOUGH!** I have no words to express how I felt.

I am sure many of you have also been hurt by Pharisees. Maybe you have been judged or rejected because you have been divorced, an immigrant, or a newcomer. Maybe you are too liberal, too conservative, or do not have a certain economic status.

Maybe you suffer silently. You judge and reject yourself because you have had an abortion or are gay. **You may have become your own Pharisee!**

I am so sorry for all of the pain you have experienced. Please forgive me because, at times, I also have been a Pharisee. Pray for those who have hurt you. Declare your forgiveness towards them, even if you don't feel it quite yet and look to your Father in heaven for confirmation on exactly who you are.

My Sisters and Brothers,

YOU ARE PRECIOUS AND LOVED IN THE SIGHT OF YOUR FATHER IN HEAVEN!

I have loved you, my people, with an everlasting love. With unfailing love I have drawn you to myself. **Jeremiah 31:3**

PRAYER ASSIGNMENT FOR WEEK 44:

Read and contemplate Psalm 139.

Relax...look back over all your journal entries.

WORDS OF ENCOURAGEMENT

Persevere. **Don't be afraid, God is with you.** *He made you...you are precious to Him.* **He has a plan for your life and it is only good!** *He said that He is a very present help in times of trouble. You can trust God.* **I know it is hard to trust right now, so ask for the grace to trust...Tell God that you are having trouble trusting.** *He is leading you through the wilderness.* **We can't understand His ways, He is God!** *Our job is to believe.* **We cannot see the future...only God can, and He promises to work ALL out for the good to those who are faithful!** *I know you have been devastated. I know that it is unfair and wrong and even a disgrace, but we are to praise and thank God in ALL things!* **We are to pray for those who hurt us and betray us. Speak the words, "I forgive ____" every time you think of what they did.** *When we obey God it gives way to so much grace.* **Read the Psalms.**

Use those Keys of Faith, Trust, Obedience, and Love. **Get into the Boot Camp...Work it!** *Call someone who you trust – someone who understands the ways of the Kingdom and ask them to pray with you.* **Stop looking around and look up!**

My Sisters and Brothers, these are the words I speak to the many hurting, broken, and sometimes, lost people who cross my path daily. I even repeat them to myself at times.

The Lord gave me a great revelation. I was given *"sight"* into the communion of saints. By this I mean that I *"saw"* Mother Mary, my Guardian Angel, my relatives, friends and even acquaintances that have passed on with my spiritual eyes. I understood that one of the reasons why we cross paths with certain people and why certain people remain in our lives is because we need to pray for them and them for us – even those that have passed on before us.

Now I know that this may seem elementary, but for me, it goes even deeper. I realized that **every person** that I have ever known or crossed paths with are of utmost importance to my life's journey. I can see that by speaking words of encouragement or simply just praying for them is ***actually my duty, part of my life's journey*** and all are ***gifts*** to me.

THE CHALLENGE

Pay attention to those around you. Listen with your heart. If you hear ***It's impossible*** try: God says, ***All things are possible*** Luke 18:27,or ***I can't go on*** try: God says, ***My grace is sufficient***, II Corinthians 12:9 & Psalm 91:15 or ***It's not worth it*** try: God says, ***It will be worth it*** Romans 8:28, or ***I can't forgive myself*** try: God says, ***I forgive you*** I John 1:9 & Romans 8:1, or: ***I feel alone*** try: God says, ***I will never leave you or forsake you*** Hebrews 13:5.

PRAYER ASSIGNMENT FOR WEEK 45:

GO OUT AND SPREAD THE GOOD NEWS! *Don't forget to write in your journal.*

WEEK 46

GOD MOMENTS

Some years ago I attended a study program for inner healing. During the study weekend, I experienced an awesome consolation in the form of a **vision**. When I say **vision** I mean that I **saw** with my spiritual eyes.

I was grieving over the loss of my dreams for the reunification of my family and without going into too much detail describing the **vision,** I will tell you that I **saw** and **heard** Mother Mary. She said, *Do not look back, Linda.*

Later that evening I shared this with the other prayer team members. After we all shared our experiences, I began talking about the deep pain and sorrow that I was going through. My friend Tricia was there.

Tricia immediately looked me straight in the eyes, pointed her finger at me and said, *What did the Blessed Mother say to you?* To which I replied, *Do not look back, Linda.*

Tricia repeated herself in that same direct manner. *What did the Blessed Mother say to you?* Again I replied, *Do not look back, Linda.* A third time she repeated the direct command. *What did the Blessed Mother say to you?* And once again I repeated, ***Do not look back, Linda!*** She then gave me a stern nod and said, ***There you have it!***

BUTTERFLIES

Now about Tricia.

She was from England so she had the cutest accent. She so loved our Lord and had a beautiful devotion to our Blessed Mother! She also loved butterflies - maybe just as much as our

Lord and Mother Mary! She wore butterfly printed tops and skirts, and when her clothes were not adorned with butterflies, she wore butterfly pins.

Tricia put butterfly barrettes in her hair. Anywhere she could place those beautiful, colorful insects, she did. Sadly, a few years ago she passed away. Upon exiting the church after the funeral mass, her family and friends witnessed a glorious sight. Hundreds of beautiful butterflies seemingly dancing all around! Oh, I must mention that it was *not* butterfly season.

CONSOLATION

Not too long ago, I had one of those moments in my journey where I felt grief again. There were multiple triggers that brought back many painful memories. Now, St. Ignatius tells us to be aware of the movements within us – consolation or desolation – to stop and ask ourselves when and why these movements started. He says that there are good and bad spirits.

The good spirits draw us closer to God and, of course, the bad spirits push us away. The bad spirits can be the devil and his demons, our dysfunctional thought and action patterns, or past experiences and traumas. St. Ignatius gave directions, rules, to help us work through these periods of desolation. I remembered one of his rules. Pray...Pray in the Psalms...Pray with the Scriptures...Just pray!

I am sure you know that when we are in desolation it can be very hard to pray. There are other rules to help us with that scenario, but I was able to pray. I went to my bed and held my rosary. I prayed and cried.

All at once I had a ***nudge*** to look up and out of the sliding glass door. And there it was - **ONE BEAUTIFUL ORANGE**

BUTTERFLY DANCING AROUND SO GRACEFULLY! Yes, it triggered my memory of my dear friend.

What did the Blessed Mother say? She said, *Do not look back, Linda; There you have it!*

Please note: It was *not* butterfly season!

PRAYER ASSIGNMENT FOR WEEK 46:

Contemplate the times in your life when you received consolation and be thankful! *Always refer to the steps on page 3.*

LIFE STORIES

I sing a song called *I'm A Miracle.* Every time I sing it I become overwhelmed at the many miracles I have been privileged to witness and *still* witness in my life!

God has been and continues to be in the business of making miracles. We have only to open our spiritual eyes, ears, hearts and minds to see them! I would like to share one such story with you...

A dear friend of mine who suffers with asthma became pregnant with her second child. Early in the pregnancy she had an asthma attack that landed her in the hospital. She was given drugs to save her life. Though they were able to save her, the doctors informed her that the drugs they administered would damage the baby. The recommendation: abortion.

Now, my friend is a faithful follower of Jesus, and she refused the abortion against the doctor's advice. She would love her baby no matter what.

Later, in the final months of her pregnancy, she had another attack. This one was more severe than the first. Again she was brought to the hospital and again treated with drugs that would save her life. Once more the doctors informed her that the type and amount of drugs she was given would harm or even kill her baby. They proceeded to listen for that little heartbeat...*no heartbeat could be heard... no movement was detected.* Sadly, they gave her the news.

Your baby has died. We are so sorry, but you need an abortion.

My friend told me that she stayed up all night and prayed...and prayed...and prayed for discernment. After many hours of prayer, she felt a little movement from the baby and was overjoyed! She had gotten her answer!

The baby was alive. In the morning she told the doctors that she knew the baby was alive, and she refused to go ahead with the abortion. The doctors took more tests and still insisted that the baby had died. They claimed that she needed to end the pregnancy for her health's sake.

She stood firm in her belief.

My Sisters and Brothers, my friend gave birth to a healthy baby boy.

MIRACLE OR MISTAKE

Some would argue that the doctors simply made a mistake. After all, they are human, and they just practice medicine. I choose to believe that God hears and answers His children and that He is not held bound to science, medicine, or time.

He Is God! **GOD HAS NO LIMITS!** If we continue to look up and not *around* we will enjoy the many blessings that God pours down upon us every day. We will be given the grace to have our spiritual eyes, ears, hearts and minds open to the many miracles that surround us each day.

PRAYER ASSIGNMENT FOR WEEK 47:

Ask the Holy Spirit to review your life with you and show you the miracles that you have been given. Give thanks and praise!

LIFE STORIES

I believe that it is very important to share what God actively does in our lives so that we are encouraged in our faith throughout our journey.

Last week I shared about my dear friend and her healthy baby. This week I want to share another story.

For a significant period of my life I *lived* in the hospital with my son who suffered with heart defects. It was the University of Miami, Jackson Memorial Hospital. At the same time I knew a family that had a son who suffered with Leukemia. They *lived* at The Children's Hospital in Miami.

We would call each other during our hospital stays and share our fears, struggles and heartaches. We were all faithful followers of Jesus and spent many hours in prayer. As the years went on their child grew worse, and the parents were finally told that there was no more hope. The cancer had spread to his spine and eventually would travel to his brain.

The parents disagreed over stopping all treatments and letting their child enjoy whatever time he had left. The mother wanted all treatments to stop, while the father firmly said, *No!*

The child began to have seizures and was eventually forced to stop all medications. The father became desperate. It was nearly Christmas.

OUR LADY OF LOURDES

Now the father had grown up in France and had gone many times to the river at Lourdes. He knew of the many miracles that Our Lady had performed for the hundreds of people who flocked there looking for cures.

In total desperation and against his wife's wishes, he booked a flight to France. You see, his wife had reconciled with the fact that their son was going to die, and she wanted to spend one last Christmas with the whole family. Needless to say, she lost the argument.

He left with their son on Christmas Eve. When he arrived in France he went straight to the river. It was early evening, and **there was not a soul in that blessed river.** This was unheard of since the river had always been congested with hundreds of people. The father picked up his son and walked into the river where he cradled him.

They spent many hours that night in the holy water... alone... praying...

For nothing is impossible with God... **Luke 1:37**

They returned home a day later. Days passed...weeks passed...months passed...years passed. Some 30 years later that little boy is a grown man, married and **CANCER-FREE**.

MY FAVORITE SONG

"NOTHING IS IMPOSSIBLE WITH GOD" by **Jose Loo**
(used with permission)

Nothing is impossible with God, Nothing is impossible with God, He is mighty and faithful, nothing is impossible with God!

Bring Him all your worries and your cares, Know that Jesus Christ is always there, He is loving and faithful, nothing is impossible with God!

PRAYER ASSIGNMENT FOR WEEK 48:

Remember a time when you knew that God had done the impossible. Then share it with someone! *I know you are in the habit of reading, praying, pondering and journaling...yay!*

AMAZING...11 months...did you realize you had gotten this far?

GOD CARES

...your Father knows what you need before you ask him.
Matthew 6:8

*O Lord, you have searched me and known me! You know when I sit down and when I rise up; you discern my thoughts from afar. You search out my path and my lying down and are **acquainted with all my ways.** Even before a word is on my tongue, behold, O Lord, you know it altogether. Behind and before You encircle me, and lay your hand upon me. Such knowledge is too wonderful for me; it is high; I cannot attain it.* **Psalm 139:1-6**

I listen to many believers who are convinced that God is in no way interested in the daily details of their lives. Their belief is that He only cares about the "big things."

For me God is **always** caring even down to the minutest detail of my sometimes mundane, daily life – **THE SMALL STUFF!** The key is for me to **let Him in... ask... thank... praise Him.**

KIND PEOPLE

Some years ago, one of my sons lost his driver's license at the beach. *Oh well, I guess you need to report it and go about getting a replacement*, I told him. However, a kind person found it and mailed it back to him!

About a year later that same son had an opportunity to tour Europe with some friends. A few months after his return home we received a package in the mail from the French embassy. It was his wallet with everything intact – money and all. Wow...how good of the people to find his wallet and bring it to the Embassy so that it could be returned all the way back to the United States!

By now you are probably wondering why I am telling this story. Well here it is...

GOD *DOES* CARE

I went to Atlanta over the Thanksgiving holiday where I LOST MY DRIVER'S LICENSE. I was agitated at the process of getting a replacement.

Then one day I prayed, *Lord, remember when my son lost his license at the beach and a kind person sent it back to him, and remember when he lost his wallet in France and another kind person brought it to the Embassy and sent the whole wallet back to him? Do you think you could speak to the person who found my license and ask them to send it back to me?*

That morning when I looked at my mail there was a letter from MARSHALLS in Atlanta. I knew at once that the Lord had answered me. There was my license! **He answered me BEFORE I had even asked.**

THE SMALL STUFF

Indeed, the very hairs of your head are all numbered. **Luke 12:7**

PRAYER ASSIGNMENT FOR WEEK 49:

Think of your daily life...your routine...the small stuff. Where can you let God in so He can show you how much He cares?

*Be still and know that I am God. **Psalm 46:10***

A COMMAND

My Sisters and Brothers in Christ, this is a **COMMAND: BE STILL... STOP... QUIET YOURSELF... QUIET YOUR MIND... TAKE A DEEP BREATH... LOOK UP, NOT AROUND!**

The command to **"be still"** comes from the stem of a Hebrew verb *raphe* meaning to be weak, let go, release. In other words: let yourself become weak. I love this because it reminds me of another Scripture that has always been one of my favorites.[21]

*But he said to me, "My grace is sufficient for you, for my power is made perfect in weakness." **2 Corinthians 12:9-11***

A CLOSER LOOK

KNOW THAT I AM GOD and MY POWER IS MADE PERFECT IN WEAKNESS*. Wow, when I stop and meditate on these two truths that are spoken from God I am humbled. I have spent too many hours, days and even years being fearful and thinking that I am responsible for just about any and everything that has gone wrong in my life. I beat myself up, in my mind of course, for my habitual fear. These are the times when I think I am God - taking on all responsibility!

I BELIEVE

I believe that God is the Creator and Ruler of the entire universe. He is the Master and is in complete control. I believe that when I *seek first the Kingdom **Matthew 6:33**...when I am still and know that God is God* all will be given to me.

I will find peace and will be delivered from fear. What is even more amazing to me is when God says; ***My power is made*** *perfect in weakness.* When I surrender to His will, His power takes over!

THANKFULNESS

Remember when I shared with you that I began to thank God for everything?

Give thanks in ALL circumstances; for this is the will of God in Christ Jesus for you. **1 Thessalonians 5:18.**

I began thanking God for my fear and spiritual weakness. Even more I began praying *Thank you, Lord for courage and strength.* It is truly amazing the growth and wisdom that I have gained in these areas of my life. I surrendered my weakness to him, and I was made **strong** spiritually.

OBEDIENCE

Remember your **OBEDIENCE** key is not about your feelings. Obedience is about listening to God! He loves you. He knows what you need before you ask. He formed you and has a plan for your life. You were made to know, love and serve the magnificent God of the universe! So, my fellow followers of Christ, **BE STILL AND KNOW THAT HE IS GOD!**

PRAYER ASSIGNMENT FOR WEEK 50:

You may still have areas within you that you are not willing to surrender to the Lord. Ask the Lord to reveal the root of the reason as to why you are not surrendering to Him. Then praise and thank Him for that reason. *My friends, remember that you are on a journey... growth to holiness takes time... don't be discouraged... keep going.*

When Jesus came to the region of Caesarea Philippi, he asked his disciples, "Who do people say the Son of Man is?" They replied, "Some say John the Baptist; others say Elijah; and still others, Jeremiah or one of the prophets." "But what about you?" he asked. "Who do you say I am?" Simon Peter answered, "You are the Messiah, the Son of the living God." **Matthew 16:13-16**

WHO DO YOU SAY THAT I AM?

Have you ever thought about what you would answer Jesus if He asked you *Who do you say that I am?*

I never really thought about what I would answer. I just kept muddling through my journey with Jesus; learning, failing, experiencing, and hopefully growing in my faith.

I learned that He is ever faithful. He is always here for me no matter the day, time or circumstance – never changing, trustworthy, and true! I experienced and continue to experience His mercy and forgiveness towards me, even when I believe I don't deserve it.

I continue to feel His love, compassion, and gentleness towards me that leads to deep healing in my soul! I live in His continual care and provision for me. I am always amazed by the many miracles He allows me to witness both in my life and in those lives of those around me. I am also humbled when He takes my sins, of which I view as "unfixable", and uses them for my good.

JESUS IS TO ME...

When I took the time to answer this question for myself, I looked over my journey and saw that **JESUS HAS BEEN** and **IS MY: CREATOR... COUNSOLER... SAVIOR... REDEEMER... HELPER... SHIELD... PROVIDER... TEACHER... COMPANION...**

STRENGTH... GUIDE... WISDOM... GRACE... TRUTH... TRUST... FORGIVER... HEALER... BELOVED... DOOR TO HEAVEN... ONLY WAY... DELIVERER... EXAMPLE... GOOD SHEPHERD... HOPE... GLORY... HOLY ONE... PRINCE OF PEACE... LOVE OF MY LIFE!

PRAYER ASSIGNMENT FOR WEEK 51:

Find a place where you could be alone and comfortable. Take a pen and your journal. Ask the Holy Spirit to be with you – show you the truth as you look back over your life and see the Lord there as you witness His presence. Understand who he was to you at that time. Write down words that describe Him.

Then tell Jesus who He is to YOU!

YOU GLOW!

When you meet **"the one"** and fall in love, there is an unmistakable glow on your face and all around you! Everyone who knows you knows that something is up! They can't help but to get excited with you when you share your feelings about your new found love.

Chances are that all who know you can't wait to meet this special person who is making a big impact in your life. You seem to be walking on air. Nothing troubles you. You feel as though you could face any and all trials life sends your way with ease. All is well with you!

As the relationship grows, things can get a little harder. You begin to see the other in all of their humanness – sometimes sinfulness – and the time comes for you to make a decision: Stay or go!

Love outweighs all, and you decide to take the plunge and stay, never to be the same again. As time goes by you start to take on each other's habits, sayings, outlook on life, etc. You see, when we hang out with someone long enough we begin to act like them! We can actually begin to look like each other!

(PS: this is why our parents didn't want us to hang with other kids who were "a bad influence!")

YOU SHOULD GLOW!

Last week you told Jesus who He is to you. You meditated on your life and saw Him there with you in many situations... loving you... caring for you... giving you strength. Even if you didn't realize it He was with you. And if you did realize it, you were with Him.

My questions for you are: *What difference does Jesus make in your life? Do you love Him? Do you have a glow on your face and all around you? Are the people who see you excited to meet the **ONE** who is making a big impact on your life?*

*When the going gets rough do you make a decision to stick with Him? If you do, do you feel empowered to face any and all trials life has to offer with ease? Do you believe that **ALL IS WELL**? Are you beginning to act and, maybe, resemble Jesus? Is your relationship with Jesus bringing changes in your life?*

My friends, if you are in a loving relationship with Jesus **YOU CAN'T HELP BUT GLOW**!

PRAYER ASSIGNMENT FOR WEEK 52:

ANSWER THE QUESTIONS IN THE ABOVE PARAGRAPH AS YOU MEDITATE ON THESE SCRIPTURES.

Whoever is not with me is against me, and whoever does not gather with me scatters. **Matthew 12:30, Luke 11:23**

Whoever does not love does not know God, because God is love. **John 4:8**

I love you, Lord, my strength. **Psalm 18:1**

Congratulations! You did it! One whole year.

Wow you are amazing! And...

You may want to do this devotion again year after year...maybe this time collectively with a group. Just remember—we are *all* on a journey to holiness...to become spiritually free. You have the Keys of Faith, Trust, Obedience and Love, along with the many tools we've discussed. You need to get into the Boot Camp and WORK IT.

Above all you have the ultimate, merciful Love of your Amazing God; His Son; Holy Spirit and His most Blessed Mother to help, heal, guide, forgive, inspire, and teach you.

I pray that the eyes of your heart may be enlightened in order that you may know the hope to which he has called you, the riches of his glorious inheritance in his holy people, and his incomparably great power for us who believe.
Ephesians 1:18-19

I am confident that He will make a

Roadway in the Wilderness for you!

-Linda Rose

Words of Thanks

By Linda Rose

Each person that I have crossed paths with has been a gift at the hand of the Almighty. To all of you who have remained with me and to whom I hold deep love for – my loving family, wonderfully talented children, faithful friends, spiritual directors and mentors – I give unending thanks to God for you. I have learned so much from you!

To those I have loved and lost: I also give unending thanks to God. I have grown ever closer to God through the suffering of that loss.

A very special thank you to my editor, Diandra Garcia, for her expertise, wise counsel and patient, loving support of this project.

Aster Zabala, my dear friend, your insight into this project has been invaluable. Bless you.

Michelle Morse, artist extraordinaire and friend. Wow....you just keep giving of your gifts for God's glory! Thank you for saying "yes" yet again!

Thank you, Derek Perez, for your artistic contribution to the book cover.

A special thanks to Alejandra Giordano for lending a hand on every project...

Kudos to Father "Happy" Hoyer for his wonderful spirit filled discernment and guidance - without whom this book would not have been born. Thank you, Father, for always helping me to look *up* and not around!

My humblest gratitude to the Blessed Mother for her loving care of my heart.

Bibliography

1. Wickham, John, S.J. Adapted from *PRAYER COMPANION'S HANDBOOK*. Quebec, Canada: Ignatian Centre Publications Montreal. Third edition, 1991.

2. KEYS TO FREEDOM, Linda Rose, co. 1999.

3. Description of Faith Key, Linda Rose and Bob Dudley, co. 2000.

4. Description of Trust Key, Linda Rose and Bob Dudley, co. 2000.

5. *The Open Bible,* Biblical Cyclopedic Index, New American Standard. Camden, New York: Thomas Nelson Publishing, Nashville.

6. *The Open Bible,* Biblical Cyclopedic Index, New American Standard. Camden, New York: Thomas Nelson Publishing, Nashville.

7. *The Open Bible,* Biblical Cyclopedic Index, New American Standard. Camden, New York: Thomas Nelson Publishing, Nashville.

8. Description of Obedience Key, Linda Rose and Bob Dudley, co. 2000.

9. Boot camp for the Kingdom of Heaven, Linda Rose, co. 2010.

10. "Letter From God" www.fathersloveletter.com copyrighted.

11. Just Like You, Linda Rose and Bob Dudley, co. 2000.

12. Lozano, Neal. *Unbound – A Practical Guide to Deliverance.* Grand Rapids, Mi: Chosen Books, a division of baker Publishing Group, 2003, 2010.

13. Bibleplaces.com.

14. Description of Love Key, Linda Rose and Bob Dudley, co. 2000.

15. Gotquestions.org.

16. *The Open Bible,* Biblical Cyclopedic Index, New American Standard. Camden, New York: Thomas Nelson Publishing, Nashville.

17. Strong, James, LL.D., S.T.D. *The New Strong's Expanded Exhausted Concordance of the Bible.* Camden, New York: Thomas Nelson Publishing, Nashville.

18. Memidex Dictionary online.

19. Therealpresence.org.

20. Merriam-Webster Dictionary online.

21. Hebrew4Christians.com.

Scriptures References include: Catholic Online, New American Standard, Bible Hub Online, The Open Bible, and English Standard Bible.

Visit my Book Store at www.lindarose.biz for merchandise with art from this book by Michelle Morse.

Look forward to my next book:
Strength for Your Journey 2 It's All About You!

Made in the USA
Columbia, SC
25 October 2017